PRENTICE HALL FOUNDATIONS OF PHILOSOPHY SERIES

P9-ELQ-152

William Alston	Philosophy of Language
David Braybrooke	Philosophy of Social Science
Roderick M. Chisholm	Theory of Knowledge, 3E
William Dray	Philosophy of History
Joel Feinberg	Social Philosophy
Frederick Ferré	Philosophy of Technology
William K. Frankena	Ethics, 2E
Martin P. Golding	Philosophy of Law
Carl Hempel	Philosophy of Natural Science
John Hick	Philosophy of Religion, 4E
Gerald C. MacCallum	Political Philosophy
D.L.C. MacLachlan	Philosophy of Perception
Wesley C. Salmon	Logic, 3E
Jerome Shaffer	Philosophy of Mind
Richard Taylor	Metaphysics, 4E

Tom L. Beauchamp, Editor

Monroe Beardsley and Elizabeth Beardsley, Founding Editors

Fourth Edition

METAPHYSICS

Richard Taylor

University of Rochester and Hartwick College

PRENTICE HALL, Englewood Cliffs, New Jersey 07632

Library of Congress Cataloging-in-Publication Data

Taylor, Richard.
  Metaphysics / Richard Taylor. — 4th ed.
    p.   cm. — (Prentice-Hall foundations of philosophy series)
  Includes bibliographical references and index.
  ISBN 0-13-567819-6
  1. Metaphysics. I. Title. II. Series.
BD111.T3   1992
110—dc20   91-17970
                                   CIP

Acquisitions Editor: Ted Bolen
Editorial/production supervision: Patricia V. Amoroso
Copy Editor: Steve Hopkins
Prepress buyer: Herb Klein
Manufacturing buyer: Patrice Fraccio

 © 1992, 1983, 1974, 1963 by Prentice-Hall, Inc.
A Simon & Schuster Company
Englewood Cliffs, New Jersey 07632

Printed in the United States of America

10 9 8 7 6 5 4 3 2 1

ISBN 0-13-567819-6

PRENTICE-HALL INTERNATIONAL (UK) LIMITED, *London*
PRENTICE-HALL OF AUSTRALIA PTY. LIMITED, *Sydney*
PRENTICE-HALL CANADA INC., *Toronto*
PRENTICE-HALL HISPANOAMERICANA, S.A., *Mexico*
PRENTICE-HALL OF INDIA PRIVATE LIMITED, *New Delhi*
PRENTICE-HALL OF JAPAN, INC., *Tokyo*
SIMON & SCHUSTER ASIA PTE. LTD., *Singapore*
EDITORA PRENTICE-HALL DO BRASIL, LTDA., *Rio de Janeiro*

To Aristotle and Xeno

Contents

CHAPTER SEVEN

Space and Time   68

CHAPTER EIGHT

The Relativity of Time and Space   77

CHAPTER NINE

Temporal Passage   80

Foundations
of Philosophy

Many of the problems of philosophy are of such broad relevance to human concerns, and so complex in their ramifications, that they are, in one form or another, perennially present. Though in the course of time they yield in part to philosophical inquiry, they may need to be rethought by each age in the light of its broader scientific knowledge and deepened ethical and religious experience. Better solutions are found by more refined and rigorous methods. Thus, one who approaches the study of philosophy in the hope of understanding the best of what it affords will look for both fundamental issues and contemporary achievements.

Written by a group of distinguished philosophers, the Foundations of Philosophy Series aims to exhibit some of the main problems in the various fields of philosophy as they stand at the present stage of philosophical history.

While certain fields are likely to be represented in most introductory courses in philosophy, college classes differ widely in emphasis, in method of instruction, and in rate of progress. Every instructor needs freedom to change his course as his own philosophical interests, the size and makeup of his class, and the needs of his students vary from year to year. The fifteen volumes in the Foundations of Philosophy Series—each complete in itself, but complementing the others—offer a new flexibility to the instructor, who can create his own textbook by combining several volumes as he wishes and by choosing different combinations at different times. Those volumes that are not used in an introductory course will be found valuable, along with other texts or collections of readings, for the more specialized upper-level courses.

Elizabeth Beardsley / *Monroe Beardsley* /   *Tom L. Beauchamp*
Temple University   Temple University   Georgetown University

Preface

It is with much satisfaction that I have seen my book continue in popularity through these many years and several revisions. Teachers of philosophy who were introduced to the subject as students through its pages now use it in their own courses, although it has undergone much change in the meantime. It was not originally intended as an introductory text, but it has become one. Some of the ideas and arguments that were first put forth in my book have now become part of the regular fare of philosophy, most notably the argument for fatalism and the theory of agency. The former has become something of a football for philosophers to kick around with their students, and the latter, including the term "theory of agency," coined by me for this book, has become part of the vocabulary of that genre of philosophy known as action theory. It is always rewarding to invent some new thing, and the reward is greater when one finds that his ideas have had a lasting impact, whether they be accepted or rejected.

In this new edition, part of the earlier discussion of space and time has been removed, as it rested upon the philosophical error of treating times as if they were things that could be referred to. In its place has been added a chapter on the relativity of time and space. Some of this chapter, together with parts of Chapter Nine, are taken from my article on the Philosophy of Time in the Collier Encyclopedia (Macmillan Publishing Company). I have also added the chapter "Metaphysics and Meaning," first published in *The Review of Metaphysics* (1987), to suggest a metaphysical basis for questions concerning the meaning of life. Grateful appreciation is herewith expressed to the editors of these sources for permission to use this material. Readers who might think it inappropriate to connect metaphysics and values, as I have done in the final chapter, should be reminded that Plato considered them inseparable, that Kant considered morality to have a metaphysics of its own, and that Spinoza called his great metaphysical treatise simply *Ethics*.

Finally, I want to thank Professor Roderick Chisholm for the cartoons appearing in Chapter Two, and Sydney Shoemaker for the example of polarity used in Chapter Twelve, having to do with an imagined exchange of brains between two persons.

RICHARD TAYLOR

Introduction

It is sometimes said that everyone has a philosophy and even that everyone has metaphysical views. Nothing could be sillier. It is true that all people have opinions, and that some of these — such as views on religion, morals, and the meaning of life — border on philosophy and metaphysics, but few people have any conception of philosophy, and fewer still have any notion of metaphysics.

William James defined metaphysics as "nothing but an unusually obstinate effort to think clearly." Not many people think like this, except where their practical interests are involved. There is no need for them to do so, and hence no inclination. Except for rare, reflective souls, people go through life just taking for granted those questions of existence, purpose, and meaning that the metaphysician finds most puzzling. What first of all claims the attention of all creatures is the need to survive and, this being once reasonably assured, the need to exist as securely as possible. All thought begins there, and most of it ends there. We are most at home when thinking of *how* to do this or that. Hence engineering, politics, and industry are quite natural to people. But metaphysics is concerned not at all with the hows of life, but only with the whys, with questions that it is perfectly easy never to ask in one's whole lifetime.

To think metaphysically is to think, without arbitrariness and dogmatism, on the most basic problems of existence. The problems are basic in the sense that they are fundamental, that much depends on them. Religion, for example, is not metaphysics; and yet if the metaphysical theory of materialism should be true, and it should thus be a fact that men have no souls, then much religion would founder on that fact. Again, moral philosophy is not metaphysics, and yet if the metaphysical theory of determinism should be true, or if the theory of fatalism should be true, many of our traditional presuppositions of morality would stand refuted by those truths. Similarly, logic is not metaphysics, and yet if it should turn out that, because of the nature of time, some assertions are neither true nor false, this would have serious implications for traditional logic.

This suggests, contrary to what is widely assumed, that metaphysics is a foundation of philosophy, and not its capstone. One's philosophical thinking, if long pursued, tends to resolve itself into basic problems of metaphysics. This is why metaphysical thought is difficult. Indeed, it would probably be true to say that the fruit of metaphysical thought is not knowledge but _understanding_. Metaphysical questions have answers, and among competing answers, not all, certainly, can be true. If someone asserts a theory of materialism and another denies that theory, then one of those two is in error; and so it is with every other metaphysical theory. Yet it can very seldom be proved and known which theory is true. Understanding, however — and sometimes a very considerable depth of it — results from seeing the obstinate difficulties in views that often seem, on other grounds, quite obviously true. It is for this reason that one can be a wise metaphysician who nevertheless suspends judgment on metaphysical views. Such a person can see all that the metaphysical dogmatist sees, and can see all the reasons for asserting what another asserts with such confidence. But unlike that other, he sees also some reasons for doubting, and thus is, like Socrates, the wiser, even in his profession of ignorance. Let readers be warned, accordingly, that whenever they hear a philosopher proclaim any metaphysical opinion with great confidence, or hear one assert that something in metaphysics is obvious, or that some metaphysical problem turns only on confusions of concepts or upon the meanings of words, then they can be quite sure that this person is still infinitely far from philosophical understanding. His views appear to him devoid of difficulties only because he stoutly refuses to see difficulties.

A metaphysical problem is inseparable from its data, for it is these that give rise to the problem in the first place. Now, _datum_ means, literally, something "given." Thus, we take as the data of a problem certain elementary beliefs of common sense which most persons are apt to hold with some conviction prior to philosophical reflection, and which they would be reluctant to abandon. They are not themselves philosophical theories, for these are the product of philosophical reflection and usually result from the attempt to reconcile certain data with each other. They are instead the starting points for theories, the things we begin with; for in order to do anything at all, we must begin with something, and cannot spend forever just getting started. "To seek proof of matters for which we already possess clearer evidence than any proof can afford," Aristotle noted, "is to confuse the better with the worse, the plausible with the implausible, and the basic with the derivative" (_Physics_, Bk. VIII, Ch. 3). Examples of metaphysical data are the beliefs you are likely to have, independent of philosophy, that you exist, that you have a body, that past things are no longer within your control, that you sometimes have a choice between alternative courses of action, that you sometimes deliberate on these, that you are growing older and will someday die, and so on. A metaphysical *problem* arises when it is found that such data do not all seem to agree with each other, and that they appear to have implications that are inconsistent with each other. The task, then, is to find some theory that is adequate to remove these conflicts.

It should perhaps be noted that data, as I am considering them, are not things that are necessarily true, nor are they self-evident. In fact, if the conflict between certain of one's common-sense beliefs is not merely apparent but real, then some of those beliefs are bound to be false, though they might nevertheless count as data until their falseness is discovered. It is this that makes metaphysics sometimes exciting; namely, that you are sometimes driven to abandon certain opinions that you had always deemed quite obvious. Nevertheless, metaphysics has to begin with something, and since it obviously cannot begin *with* things that are proved, it must begin with things that are believed; and the confidence with which you hold your metaphysical theories can be no greater than the confidence you repose in the data upon which they rest.

Now the intellects of people are not as strong as their wills, and they generally believe whatever they want to believe, particularly when those beliefs reflect upon their own worth among others and the value of their endeavors. *Wisdom* is thus not what they first of all seek. They seek, instead, the justification for what they happen to cherish. It is not surprising, then, that beginners in philosophy, and even those who are not beginners, have a strong inclination to hold fast to some theory that appeals to them, in the face of conflicting data, and sometimes to deny that the data are true just for this reason. This hardly promotes wisdom. Thus, it is not uncommon to find someone who, say, wants badly to believe in the theory of determinism, and who from this desire simply denies the truth of any data that conflict with it. The data, in other words, are simply adjusted to the theory, rather than the theory to the data. But it must still be insisted that it is the data, and not the theory, that one should begin with; for if we do not begin with some fairly plausible presuppositions, where are we going to get the theory, other than just embracing what our hearts desire? We may sooner or later have to abandon some of our common-sense data, but when we do, it should be in deference to certain other common-sense beliefs that we are even more reluctant to relinquish, and not in deference to philosophical theories that are appealing.

You are therefore exhorted, in pursuing the thoughts that follow, to suspend judgment concerning the final truths of things — since probably neither you nor anyone else knows what these are — and to content yourself with appreciating the problems of metaphysics. This is the first and always the most difficult step. The rest of the truth, if you are ever lucky enough to receive any of it, will come from within you, if it ever comes at all, and not from the reading of books.

The discussion that follows constitutes an introduction — literally, a "leading in" — to metaphysics. It is not a survey of prevailing views, and you will search in vain for the names of great thinkers or summaries of opinions they held. Metaphysical problems are elicited, and you are invited simply to think on them along the lines suggested. It is for this reason that, in developing problems most closely associated with the *self* or *person* and its powers, particularly in the first three chapters, the often stylistically objectionable first person singular "I" is frequently employed, after the manner of Descartes' *Meditations*. You should understand that the ideas presented in this form are intended as your own, and not as autobiographical reflections of the author.

CHAPTER ONE

The Need for
Metaphysics

There are many things one can do without. Among them are even things fool-
ish persons devote their life's energy to winning. One can do without wealth,
for example, and be no less happy than if one had it. One can do without position, status, or power over others, and be no less happy, certainly no less
human. Very likely, without these one will be more human, more the kind of
being that nature or God, whatever gave being in the first place, intended.
Indeed, such things as these — possessions, power, fame, which mean so
much to the unreflective — appear on examination to be no more than des-
perate attempts to give meaning to a life that is without meaning. They reflect
the vain notion that one's worth can be protected, even enhanced, by raven-
ous accumulation, if not of gold, then of its modern equivalents. When this
fails, the pursuit of such things as often as not becomes little more than the response to the need to have something to do. Few people are able to sit still,
much less to sit still and think; and when enforced idleness threatens, most
people begin to plan for travel to distant places, for purchases to be made, or
for pictures to take in far-off lands — in short, for something to do. Just the
going and coming will keep them busy for a while, get them through that
much of life, and take their minds off things by presenting a variety and nov-
elty to their sense organs. Perhaps people are, as the ancients declared, rational animals; but if this is so, it is so only in the sense that they are uniquely
capable of reason, contemplation, and thought, not that they spend much of
their lives at it. We still share with the rest of animate creatures restless needs
and cravings that drive us perpetually to movement. Aristotle's dictum that
life is motion surely applies to our own lives. It is what we share with other

animals that is most apparent, not the elusive qualities that set us apart. The same philosopher associated reason and thought and contemplation with the gods. He did not first look to mortals for the expression of intelligence — except, interestingly, to those few of its specimens gifted with the love for philosophy and metaphysics, and whose happiness he therefore compared with that of the gods.

LOVE AND NATURE

There are, however, some things one cannot do without, at least not without deep suffering and the diminishing of one's nature. Among these is the love and approbation of at least a few of one's fellow beings. Lacking these, one seeks the semblance of them in the form of feigned affection, pretended deference, awe, and sometimes fear. It is astonishing that these counterfeits will so often do, will even seem to give significance to people's lives. Yet we see on every side that this is in fact so. The explanation is of course not in the worth of these things themselves but in the depth of the need people vainly seek to satisfy through the means of such things.

Another need that cannot be destroyed or left unmet without great damage — one of which metaphysicians have often been acutely aware — is the love for nature and the feeling of our place within it. Without this we become machines, grinding out our days and hours to that merciful end when death imposes the peace we have never been able to find for ourselves. Children easily think of themselves as things apart, virtual centers of reality about which the whole of nature turns, to whose wants everything ministers. One who loves nature rises above this paltry conception of his own being and becomes sensitive to his identity with the whole of reality, which is without beginning or end. This partially explains the difficulty many persons have in fathoming metaphysics. It is not that it is so difficult, but that it is approached from the wrong point of view — from a childhood mentality, from the standpoint of one who finds oneself always at the center of the stage, all else being a vast thing without spirit or soul. It is hardly the frame of mind in which to understand a Plato, a Buddha, or a Spinoza.

METAPHYSICS AND WISDOM

Still another such need, strangely, is the need for metaphysics itself. We cannot live as fully rational beings without it. This does not mean that metaphysics promises the usual rewards that a scientific knowledge of the world so stingily withholds. It does not promise freedom, God, immortality, or anything of the sort. It offers neither a rational hope nor the knowledge of these. Metaphysics, in fact, promises no *knowledge* of anything. If knowledge itself is what you seek, be grateful for empirical science, for you will never find it in metaphysics.

Then what is its reward? What does metaphysics offer that is in its power alone to give? What, that this boundless world cannot give even to the richest and most powerful — that it seems, in fact, to withhold from these more resolutely than from the poor and the humble? Its reward is wisdom. Not boundless wisdom, not invincible truth, which must be left to the gods, not a great understanding of the cosmos or of man, but wisdom, just the same; and it is as precious as it is rare.

What, then, is so good about it? What is wisdom worth if it does not fulfill our deep cravings, such as the craving for freedom, for gods to worship, for a bit more of life than material nature seems to promise? What makes it worth seeking at all?

The first reward of such wisdom is, negatively, that it saves one from the numberless substitutes that are constantly invented and tirelessly peddled to the simple-minded, usually with stunning success, because there is never any dearth of customers. It saves us from these glittering gems and baubles, promises and dogmas and creeds that are worth no more than the stones under one's feet. Fools grasp, at the slightest solicitation, for any specious substitute that offers a hope for the fulfillment of their desires, the products of brains conditioned by greed and competition, no matter how stupid, sick, or destructive these may be. Many persons, in response to the deep need to be loved, of which we have spoken, have felt themselves transformed by a mere utterance — such as, for example, "Jesus loves you!" — an assurance that is cheaply and insincerely flung at them by ambitious evangelists. The instant conviction that such blandishments sometimes produce is uncritically taken to be a sign of their certain truth, when in fact they signify nothing more than a need that demands somehow to be met, by whatever means. Again, many persons can banish at will, even before it is really felt, the dread and the objective certainty of their own inevitable destruction. For this comfort they need nothing more than the mere reminder of some promise expressed in a text of ancient authority, or some holy book, or even the simple declamation of a clever and manipulative preacher. In this way does the religion of faith, perverting everything and turning the world upside down, serve as the cheap metaphysics, not of the poor, but of those impoverished in spirit and wanting in wisdom, some of whom bask in a blaze of worldly glory. Such religion, substituting empty utterance for thought, is not the religion of the metaphysical mind or of those who love God and nature first and themselves as a reflection of this.

Where religion can make no headway, in the mind of the skeptic, ideology can sometimes offer some sort of satisfaction to much the same need. Thus many persons spend their lives in a sandcastle, a daydream, in which every answer to every metaphysical question decorates its many mansions. The whole thing is the creation of their brains, or worse, of their needs — it is an empty dream, for nothing has been created except illusions. Such dreams are not metaphysics but the substitute for metaphysics. They illustrate again how one can live without metaphysics only if some substitute, however specious, is supplied, and this is testimony to the deep need for it.

What am I? What is this world, and why is it such? Why is it not like the moon — bleak, barren, hostile, meaningless? How can such a thing as this be? What is this brain; does it think? And this craving or will, whence does it arise? Is it free? Does it perish with me, or not? Is it perhaps everlasting? What is death — and more puzzling still, what is birth? A beginning? An ending? And life — is it a clockwork? Does the world offer no alternatives? And if so, does it matter? What can one think about the gods, if anything at all? Are there any? Or is nature itself its own creator, and the creator of me; both cradle and tomb, both holy and mundane, both heaven and hell?

The answers to such things are not known. They never will be. It is pointless to seek the answers in the human brain, in science, or in the pages of philosophy and metaphysics. But they will be sought, just the same, by everyone who has a brain, by the stupid as well as the learned, by the child, the adult, by whoever can look at the world with wonder. False and contrived answers will always abound. There will always be those who declare that they *know* the answers to these things, that they "found" these answers in some religious experience, in some esoteric book of "divine" authorship, or in something occult. They do not *find* them; they find nothing at all except the evaporation of their need to go on asking questions, and of their fears of what the answers to those questions could turn out to be. They find, in other words, a comfort born of ignorance.

So the need of metaphysics endures. No one will shake it off. Metaphysics will be shunned by most people, always, because its path is not easy and no certain treasures lie at the end. Its poor cousins will be chosen in preference, because they offer everything at no cost — a god to worship who has set us apart from the rest of creation and guarantees each an individual immortality, and a will that is free to create a destiny.

People will always choose substitutes for metaphysics. Because of the indestructible need for it, they will accept anything, however tawdry, however absurd, as a surrogate. Yet it is only metaphysics that, while preserving one in the deepest ignorance, while delivering up not the smallest grain of knowledge of anything, will nevertheless give that which alone is worth holding on to, repudiating whatever promises something better. For metaphysics promises wisdom, a wisdom sometimes inseparable from ignorance, but whose glow is nevertheless genuine, from itself, not borrowed, and not merely the reflection of our bright and selfish hopes.

CHAPTER TWO

Persons and Bodies

Sometimes the simplest and most obvious distinctions give rise to the profoundest intellectual difficulties, and things most commonplace in our daily experience drive home to us the depths of our ignorance. People have fairly well fathomed the heavens, so that perhaps nothing counts as surer knowledge than astronomy, the science of the things most distant from us, and yet the grass at our feet presents impenetrable mysteries. In like manner, our knowledge of human history, of cultures remote in time and distance, fills volumes, and yet we are all, each of us, bewildered by that one being that is closest to us, namely, the self, as soon as we ask the most elementary questions. And oddly, it seems that the simplest question you can ask about yourself — namely, "What am I?" — is the very hardest to answer, and nonetheless the most important. You can ask what many other things are, such as a tree, a drop of water, or a machine, and be quite certain that your answers, though incomplete, are nonetheless not wholly wrong. But when you ask what you yourself are, what you are in your innermost nature, or when you ask what is that "I" with which you are so intimately concerned and which is for you the very center of the universe, then you are bewildered, and must fall back on philosophical speculations of the most difficult sort.

It is, moreover, this simple and basic question that has the greatest philosophical ramifications. All morals, religion, metaphysics, and law turn upon it. Law and morality, for example, presuppose the existence of moral agents who have responsibilities and are capable of incurring guilt. But obviously, certain kinds of things can have responsibilities, and certain others cannot; and if people are in fact beings of the latter kind, then morality and law, as traditionally conceived, are nonsense. Again, many religions presuppose that people are spiritual beings, capable of surviving the destruction of their bodies in death. If a person is in fact nothing of the sort, then those religions rest upon a misconception. It is thus imperative that we try to find some answer to this basic and simple question.

Now, while most people are, throughout their lives, almost wholly absorbed in practical ends, in the pursuit of the objects of their desires, so that their thoughts are perpetually directed to outward things, reflective people are nonetheless sometimes led to consider their own being, which is then apt to seem to them mysterious. Thus, when someone who was well known and perhaps loved dies, it is quite natural to think that this person is not the same thing as those remains that sink into the grave, for it is not these that were so known and loved. A religious person in these circumstances is therefore likely to speak not of death but of departing. Again, when you rejoice in your achievements, particularly if they seem to have some profound moral significance, or when you regret your failures, you are not likely to suppose that your body, or any part of it, such as your nervous system, is the object of such attitudes. Instead, it is that part of you which makes you distinctively *personal* that you rejoice in or blame, for you congratulate or reproach *yourself*. And so it is with all distinctively human relations, like love and friendship, which seem to unite people, and not with simply natural physical bodies, such as are the subject matter of physical science.

THE REALITY OF THE SELF AND THE BODY

However unsure I may be of the nature of myself and of the relation of myself to my body, I can hardly doubt the reality of either. Whether I am identical with my body, or whether I am a spirit, or soul, or perhaps only a collection of thoughts and feelings — whatever I am, I cannot doubt my own being, cannot doubt that I am part of the world, even prior to any philosophical reflection on the matter. For surely if I know anything at all, as presumably I do, then I know that I exist. There seems to be nothing I could possibly know any better. And this is, of course, quite consistent with my great ignorance as to the nature of that self of whose existence I feel so assured.

I know, further, that I have a body. I may have learned this from experience, in the same way that I have learned of the existence of innumerable other things, or I may not have; it is, in any case, something I surely know. I may also have only the vaguest conception, or even a totally erroneous one, of the relationship between myself and my body; I can nevertheless no more doubt the reality of the one than the other. I may also be, as I surely am, quite ignorant of the nature and workings of my body and even of many of its parts, but no such ignorance raises the slightest doubt of its reality.

Now, what is the connection between these, between myself and my body? Just what relationship am I affirming by "have," when I say with such confidence that I have a body? Abstractly, there seem to be just three general possibilities. In the first place, my having a body might consist simply in the *identity* of myself with my body, or of my *being* a body. Or, second, it might amount to *possession*, such that my having a body consists essentially in this body's being among the various other things that I own or possess, it being at the same time, perhaps, in some way unique among these. Or, finally, there may be some special, perhaps highly metaphysical relationship between the two, such as that I as a person am one thing, my body another quite different thing, the two being somehow connected to each other in a special way, appropriately expressed by the assertion that the one *has* the other.

Now there are great difficulties in all these suggestions, and, under the third, numerous special theories are possible, as we shall see. We had best, however, begin with the simplest view, to see, then, whether any of the others are any better.

MATERIALISM

I know that I have a body, and that this is a material thing, though a somewhat unusual and highly complicated one. There would, in fact, be no other reason for calling it my body, except to affirm that it is entirely material, for nothing that is not matter could possibly be a part of my body. Now if my having a body consists simply in the identity of myself with my body, then it follows that I *am* this body, and nothing more. Nor would the affirmation of the identity of myself with my body be at all inconsistent with saying that I have a body, for we often express the relationship of identity in just this way. Thus, one might correctly say of a table that it *has* four legs and a top, or of a bicycle that it *has* two wheels, a frame, a seat, and handlebars. In such cases, no one would suppose that the table or the bicycle is one thing, and its parts or "body" another, the two being somehow mysteriously connected. The table or the bicycle just *is* its parts, suitably related. So likewise, I might just *be* the totality of my bodily parts, suitably related and all functioning together in the manner expressed by saying that I am a living body, or a living, material animal organism.

This materialistic conception of a person has the great advantage of simplicity. We do know that there are bodies, that there are living animal bodies, and that some of these are in common speech called *people*. A person is, then, on this view, nothing mysterious or metaphysical, at least as regards the *kind* of thing he or she is.

A consequence of this simplicity is that we need not speculate upon the relationship between one's body and one's mind, or ask how the two are connected, or how one can act upon the other, all such questions being rendered senseless within the framework of this view, which in the first place denies that we are dealing with two things. The death of the animal organism — which is, of course, an empirical fact and not subject to speculation — will, moreover, be equivalent to the destruction of the person, consisting simply in the cessation of those functions that together constitute one's being alive. Hence, the fate of a person is simply, on this view, the fate of his body, which is ultimately a return to the dust whence he sprang. This alleged identity of oneself with one's body accounts, moreover, for the solicitude every person has for his body, and for its health and well-being. If a person is identical with his body, then any threat to the latter is a threat to himself, and he must view the destruction of it as the destruction of himself. And such, in fact, does seem to be everyone's attitude, whatever may be their philosophical or religious opinions. Again, the distinction that everyone draws between himself and other people, or himself and other things, need be no more than the distinction between one body and others. When I declare that some foreign object —a doorknob, for instance, or a shoe — is no part of myself, I may be merely making the point that it is no part of my body. I would, surely, be more hesitant in declaring that my hand, or my brain and nervous system, which are physical objects, are no parts of me.

Such a conception has nevertheless always presented enormous difficulties, and these have seemed so grave to most philosophers that almost any theory, however absurd when examined closely, has at one time or another seemed to them preferable to materialism. Indeed, the difficulties of materialism are so grave that, for some persons, they need only to be mentioned to render the theory unworthy of discussion.

THE MEANING OF "IDENTITY"

By "identity" the materialist must mean a strict and total identity of himself and his body, nothing less. Now to say of anything, X, and anything, Y, that X and Y are identical, or that they are really one and the same thing, one must be willing to assert of X anything whatever that he asserts of Y, and vice versa. This is simply a consequence of their identity, for if there is anything whatever that can be truly asserted of any object X but cannot be truly asserted of some object Y, then it logically follows that X and Y are two different things, and not the same thing. In saying, for instance, that the British wartime prime minister and Winston Churchill are one and the same person, one commits himself to saying of either whatever he is willing to say of the other — such as that he lived to a great age, smoked cigars, was a resolute leader, was born at Blenheim Palace, and so on. If there were any statement whatever that was true of, say, Mr. Churchill, but not true of the wartime prime minister, then it would follow that Mr. Churchill was not the wartime prime minister, that we are here referring to two different men.

The question can now be asked, then, whether there is anything true of me that is not true of my body, and vice versa. There are, of course, ever so many things that can be asserted indifferently of both me and my body without absurdity. For instance, we can say that I was born at such and such place and time, and it is not the least odd to say this of my body as well. Or we can say that my body now weighs exactly so many pounds, and it would be just as correct to give this as my weight; and so on.

But now consider more problematical assertions. It might, for instance, be true of me at a certain time that I am morally blameworthy or praiseworthy. Can we then say that my body or some part of it, such as my brain, is in exactly the same sense blameworthy or praiseworthy? Can moral predicates be applied without gross incongruity to any physical object at all? Or suppose I have some profound wish or desire, or some thought — the desire, say, to be in some foreign land at a given moment, or to have the thoughts of the Homeric gods. It seems at least odd to assert that my body, or some part of it, wishes that it were elsewhere, or has thoughts of the gods. How, indeed, can any purely physical state of any purely physical object ever be a state that is *for* something, or *of* something, in the way that my desires and thoughts are such? And how, in particular, could a purely physical state be in this sense *for* or *of* something that is not real? Or again, suppose that I am religious and can truly say that I love God and neighbor, for instance. Can I without absurdity say that my body or some part of it, such as my foot or brain, is religious, and loves God and neighbor? Or can one suppose that my being religious, or having such love, consists simply in my body's being in a certain state, or behaving in a certain way? If I claim the identity of myself with my body, I must say all these odd things; that is, I must be willing to assert of my body, or some part of it, everything I assert of myself. There is perhaps no logical absurdity or clear falseness in speaking thus of one's corporeal frame, but such assertions as these are at least strange, and it can be questioned whether, as applied to the body, they are even still meaningful.

The disparity between bodily and personal predicates becomes even more apparent, however, if we consider epistemological predicates involved in statements about belief and knowledge. Thus, if I believe something — believe, for instance, that today is February 31 — then I am in a certain state; the state, namely, of having a certain belief, which is in this case necessarily a false one. Now, how can a physical state of any physical object be identical with that? And how, in particular, can anything be a *false* physical state of an object? The physical states of things, it would seem, just *are*, and one cannot even think of anything that could ever distinguish one such state from another as being either true or false. Physiologists might give a complete physical description of a brain and nervous system at a particular time, but they could never distinguish some of those states as true and others as false, nor would they have any idea what to look for if they were asked to do this. At least, so it would certainly seem.

PLATONIC DUALISM

It is this sort of reflection that has always led metaphysicians and theologians to distinguish radically between the mind or soul of a man and his body, ascribing properties to the mind that are utterly different in kind from those exhibited by the body; properties that, it is supposed, could not be possessed by any body, just because of its nature as a physical object.

The simplest and most radical of such views *identifies* the person or self with a soul or mind and declares its relationship to the body to be the almost accidental one of mere occupancy, possession, or use. Thus Plato, and many mystical philosophers before and after him, thought of the body as a veritable prison of the soul, a gross thing of clay from which the soul one day gladly escapes, to live its own independent and untrammeled existence, much as a bird flees its cage or a snake sheds its skin. A person, thus conceived, is a nonmaterial substance — a *spirit*, in the strictest sense — related to an animal body as possessor to thing possessed, tenant to abode, or user to thing used. A person *has* a body only in the sense that he, perhaps temporarily, occupies, owns, or uses a body, being all the while something quite distinct from it and having, perhaps, a destiny quite different from the melancholy one that is known sooner or later to overtake the body.

This dualism of mind and body has been, and always is, firmly received by millions of unthinking people partly because it is congenial to the religious framework in which their everyday metaphysical opinions are formed, and partly, no doubt, because everyone wishes to think of himself as something more than just one more item of matter in the world. Wise philosophers, too, speak easily of the attributes of the mind as distinct from those of the body, thereby sundering the two once and for all. Some form of dualism seems, in fact, indicated by the metaphysical, moral, and epistemological difficulties of materialism, which are, it must be confessed, formidable indeed.

But whatever difficulties such simple dualism may resolve, it appears to raise others equally grave. For one thing, it is not nearly as simple as it seems. Whatever a partisan of such a view might say of the simplicity of the mind or soul, a *person* is nonetheless, on this view, *two* quite disparate things, a mind and a body, each having almost nothing in common and only the flimsiest connection with the other. This difficulty, once it is acutely felt, is usually minimized by conceiving of a person in his true self as nothing but a mind, and representing his body as something ancillary to this true self, something that is not really any part of him at all but only one among the many physical objects that he happens to possess, use, or what not, much as he possesses and uses various other things in life. His body does, to be sure, occupy a preeminent place among such things, for it is something without which he would be quite helpless; but this renders it no more a part or whole of his true self or person than any other of the world's physical things.

Possession, however, is essentially a social concept, and sometimes a strictly legal one. Something counts as one of my possessions by virtue of my title to it, and this is something conferred in accordance with conventions and laws. Thus does a field or a building count as one of my possessions. But a certain animal body, which I identify as mine, is not mine in any sense such as this. My dominion over my body arises from no human conventions or laws and is not alterable by them. The body of a slave, though it may be owned by another man in the fullest sense of ownership that is reflected in the idea of possession, is nevertheless the slave's body in a metaphysical sense. And, in this sense, it could not possibly be the body of his master. One has, moreover, a solicitude for his body wholly incommensurate with his concern for any treasure, however dear. The loss of the latter is regarded as no more than a loss, though perhaps a grave one, while the abolition of one's body cannot be regarded as the mere loss of something dearly held, but is contemplated as an appalling and total calamity.

The ideas of occupancy or use do not express the relation of mind and body any better. *Occupancy,* for instance, is a physical concept; one thing occupies another by being in or upon it. But the mind, on this view, is no physical thing, and no sense can be attached to its resting within or upon any body; the conception is simply ridiculous. Nor do you simply *use* your body the way you use implements and tools. You do, to be sure, sometimes use your limbs and other parts, over which you have voluntary control, in somewhat the manner in which you use tools; but many of your bodily parts, including some that are vital, the very existence of which may be unknown to you, are not within your control at all. They are nonetheless parts of your body. Artificial devices, too, like hearing aids, eyeglasses, and the like, do not in the least become parts of one's body merely by being used, even in the case of someone who can barely do without them. They are merely things worn or used. Nor can you say that your body is that physical being in the world upon which you absolutely depend for your continuing life, for there are many such things. You depend on the sun, for instance, and the air you breathe, and without these you would perish as certainly as if deprived of your heart. Yet no one regards the sun or the air around him as any part of his body.

A person does not, then, *have* a body in the way in which he has anything else at all, and any comparison of the body to a material possession or instrument is about as misleading as likening it to a chamber in which one is more or less temporarily closeted. The connection between yourself and your body is far more intimate and metaphysical than anything else you can think of. One's body is at least a part of himself, and is so regarded by everyone. Yet it is not merely a part, as the arm is part of the body; and we are so far without any hint of how the mind and the body are connected.

A PLETHORA OF THEORIES

Clearly, if you so much as *distinguish* between your body and your mind and treat these as two different things, you raise problems of such enormous difficulty that any theory, however bizarre, is apt to appear plausible if it offers some hope of removing them. Just once sunder body and mind, and enough problems are created to keep philosophers at work for generations. There is, in fact, hardly any theory so bizarre that it has not at one time or another found strong defenders among the most able thinkers. Just as materialists, for example, in the effort to obviate the necessity of connecting mind and matter, have simply denied the existence of minds, so also have *idealists* denied the existence of matter, maintaining that all bodies, including one's own, exist only as ideas in some mind. Others, unwilling to deny the existence either of minds or of bodies, have suggested that the connection between them is that of cause and effect, that my body acts upon my mind and my mind upon my body, and that just this causality is what connects and unites the two into one person. This is the theory of *interactionism*. Others, unable to see how a mind, which is not material, can have physical effects, have maintained that the body acts upon the mind to produce consciousness, thought, and feeling, but that the mind itself has no physical effects, which is the theory of *epiphenomenalism*. Still others, finding the same difficulty in the idea of the body's acting upon the mind as in the idea of the mind's acting upon the body, have suggested that there is really only one kind of substance, and that what we call "mind" and "body" are simply two aspects of this. This is called the *double aspect* theory. Again, to meet the same difficulty, it has been supposed that mind and body, being different substances, never act upon each other, but the histories of each are nevertheless such that there *seems* to be such a causal connection. This is the theory of *parallelism*. It has even been suggested that this parallelism is wrought by God, who, in creating a person, arranges in advance that his mental and physical histories should always be in close correspondence without interacting, in the manner of a *pre-established harmony*. Alternatively, it has been seriously maintained that all of one's mental life is caused, from moment to moment, by God, who sees to it that this mental life is in close correspondence with what is going on in the body. This theory has come down to us under the name of *occasionalism*.

Most of these theories are not deserving of serious attention, but they are mentioned to give some intimation of the difficulty of our problem. A seemingly outrageous theory can cease to seem outrageous if the difficulties it promises to remove are enormous ones, and worth almost any price to get rid of. Of all these theories we shall in the next chapters consider only those of interactionism and epiphenomenalism, which are the only ones that are now widely maintained, except for materialism, to which we shall then return. Meanwhile, the theories just mentioned are graphically compared in Roderick Chisholm's accompanying cartoons.

INTERACTIONISM

EPIPHENOMENALISM

MATERIALISM

IDEALISM

Substances

DOUBLE ASPECT THEORY

mind   Body

PARALLELISM

God is always controlling both our minds + bodies

OCCASIONALISM

PRE-ESTABLISHED HARMONY

histories in correspondence by God

RMC

CHAPTER THREE

Interactionism

Because I can hardly deny that I exist, and that I have a body which is at least a part of myself, then I must either affirm the identity of myself with my body, according to the materialistic conception described earlier, or else affirm that I am two things — a mind that has a body and, equally, a body that has a mind. Nothing else is consistent with the data with which we began.

Now, the simplest and most common way of expressing the relation between a body and a mind, so that they together constitute a person, is to say that they interact; that is, they causally act, each upon the other. More fully we can say that while the mind of a person is not a physical thing, events that transpire within it sometimes have causal consequences or effects within the body. Conversely, although the body of a person is clearly not a mental or nonphysical thing, the events that occur within it, particularly within the nervous system and brain, sometimes have causal consequences or effects within the mind or consciousness. The body and mind of an individual person, accordingly, are whatever body and mind are so related. *My* body is that physical object that is within my immediate control, that is, that physical object, alone among all the others in the universe, that events within my mind are capable of affecting directly; and similarly, *my* mind is that mind, among all the others in the universe, that events within my body are capable of affecting directly. This, according to the view we are now considering, is what is meant by saying of a given body that it is mine, or that I *have* a certain body. What *I* am, accordingly, is a certain composite of body and mind that thus interact with each other.

Now, this conception of a person, which is very old and familiar, appears in some measure confirmed by the manner in which we often describe certain of our experiences. Thus, when there is some disorder in my body, such as a severely decayed tooth, or a laceration in the skin, it appears clearly to be the *cause* of a purely subjective, unobservable state called *pain*. And the fact that such a pain is subjective and unobservable to anyone else suggests that it is not, like the decay or the laceration, a state of my body at all, but rather something mental. Thus a dentist can observe the decay, and a physiologist can describe in some detail the changes within my nerves, which are further bodily changes, that this decay gives rise to; but both the dentist and physiologist are necessarily barred from ever observing the pain that is the ultimate effect of these bodily changes, just because it is not, like these, a bodily change at all. Instruments of increasing refinement, such as microscopes and the like, can pick out more and more bodily changes hitherto unobserved. Their inability ever to pick out a pain for observation does not result from their inadequacy as instruments of observation but from metaphysical considerations. A pain cannot, along with physical changes of whatever minuteness, be observed by any devices whatsoever, simply because it is not a physical change at all but a mental one, and for that reason unobservable. The only person who can become aware of a pain or any other state of mind or mental event is that person in whose mind it occurs, and his awareness of it is, of course, immediate. Even he cannot observe it in the same way that he observes any physical object, state, or change, whether in his own body or some other.

Similarly, it is not uncommon to think of purely mental changes having observable effects within the body. Fear, for example, is a subjective mental state that produces perspiration and other bodily changes. Again, the mere thought of food sometimes produces salivation, and some persons' hands can be made to perspire by the mere thought of high places and precarious situations. Voluntary activity, moreover, is often represented as bodily behavior having among its causes one's choices, decisions, intentions, or volitions, and these are psychological in nature and hence unobservable by any outsider. Though someone were able to witness *all* the inner and outer workings of my body, in all its minutest parts, and accurately describe *all* the physical and chemical changes occurring therein, that person could not, it is often alleged, ever pick out one of my volitions or choices. He could see the *effects* of these in the form of gross and subtle bodily changes; but he could not *see* the choices or volitions that cause these effects, simply because they are not bodily changes to begin with. They are changes within the mind, and for that reason metaphysically incapable of being observed.

THE REFUTATION OF THIS

However natural it may seem to conceive a person in such terms, as a dual complex of two wholly disparate things, body and mind, it is nonetheless an impossible conception, on the simplest metaphysical grounds. For on this view, the body and the mind *are* wholly disparate things, so that any bodily change wrought by the mind or by some nonphysical occurrence transpiring therein is a change that lies quite outside the realm of physical law. This means that human behavior is veritably miraculous. Now, some people, reflecting on the old dictum that anything, after all, can cause anything, might be willing to accept this consequence, thus broadly stated, pointing out at the same time that human nature is, after all, somewhat mysterious. Nevertheless, when we come to some precise instance of the alleged interaction of body and mind, as conceived by this theory, we find that we are dealing with something that is not merely mysterious but wholly unintelligible.

Consider some clear and simple case of what would on this theory constitute the action of the mind upon the body. Suppose, for example, that I am dwelling in my thought upon high and precarious places, all the while knowing that I am really safely ensconced in my armchair. I imagine, perhaps, that I am picking my way along a precipice and visualize the destruction that awaits me far below in case I make the smallest slip. Soon, simply as the result of these thoughts and images, which are not for a moment attended by any belief that I am in the slightest danger, perspiration appears on the palms of my hands. Now here is surely a case, if there is any, of something purely mental, unobservable, and wholly outside the realm of physical nature bringing about observable physical changes. We do not have in this situation an instance of physical stimuli from the environment causing physical reactions in the organism, for the actual stimuli are the normal ones of my room and armchair, and these do not change. The only significant change is in my thoughts and images, which are directly in the control of my will and are followed by the physical effect on my hands. Here, then, one wants to say, the mind acts upon the body, producing perspiration.

But what actually happens, alas, is not nearly so simple as this. To say that thoughts in the mind produce sweat on the hands is to simplify the situation so grossly as hardly to approximate any truth at all of what actually happens. A complete account of the complexities involved here cannot be given, for it is unknown, but some elaboration is possible, in the light of which it is far from obvious that we have, even in this case, an instance of the mind acting on the body.

The perspiration, everyone knows, is secreted by tiny, complex glands in the skin. They are caused to secrete this substance, not by any mind acting on them, but by the contraction of little unstriated muscles. These tiny muscles are composed of numerous minute cells, wherein occur chemical reactions of the most baffling complexity. It is believed, however, that the energy required for their activity is derived from the oxidation of fatty acids, or perhaps of acetoacetate. Their contraction in any case generates electrical current of small but measurable amounts. It might be supposed that these muscles are innervated by the mind, which by some mysterious alchemy produces the chemical reactions within their cells; but this, even if it makes any sense, is certainly not true. The muscles are activated by hormones produced by the adrenal medulla in response to impulses of the autonomic nervous system, probably by the hormones epinephrine or norepinephrine, or, more likely in the present case, by an epinephrine-like substance that is produced in minute quantities by adrenergic fibers, that is, certain post-ganglionic neurons of the sympathetic nervous system. Where this substance originally comes from is apparently not known, but it cannot be doubted that it is a physical substance — indeed, its chemical formula is known — and that it is synthesized in the body. It has, in any case, no mental or extraphysical origin. It is the activity of the neurons of the sympathetic nervous system that leads to the production of this epinephrine-like substance by the adrenergic fibers. How impulses are propagated by these neurons is also not entirely understood, but it seems to be somewhat as follows: Stimulation of a neuron increases the permeability of the neuron membrane, causing a diffusion of sodium ions into the neuron itself, so that the neuron within becomes positively charged with respect to the outside, with a resultant flow of current. Such currents are easily detected and fairly accurately measured by a physiologist. The diffused fibers of the sympathetic nervous system coalesce and center about two chains of ganglia that are arranged along the sides of the spinal cord. Unlike the neurons of the parasympathetic nervous system, those of the sympathetic nervous system synapse near these ganglia. The nerve impulse is transmitted across the synapse by the help of acetylcholine, a fairly well-known substance that is believed to be produced by the terminal fibrils of the nerves. The cells of the spinal ganglia are supplied by preganglionic neuron fibers arising from the spinal cord. These, in turn, connect eventually, and in the most dreadfully complicated way, with the hypothalamus, a delicate part of the brain that is centrally involved in the emotional reactions of the organism, and in the so-called homeostasis of the organism, i.e., in the self-regulation of its internal environment How it operates to effect this internal balance, and to originate those impulses that lead to such diverse effects as sweating, increased pulse, and so on is quite unclear, but it is not seriously considered by those who do know something about it that mental events must be included in the description of its operations. The hypothalamus, in turn, is closely connected with the cortex and subcortical areas of the brain, so that physical and chemical changes within these areas produce corresponding physical effects within the hypothalamus, which in turn, by a series of physical processes whose complexity has only barely been suggested, produces such remote effects as the secretion of perspiration on the surface of the hands.

Such, in the barest outline, is something of the chemistry and physics of emotional perspiration. What is involved is an enormously complex causal chain of physical processes. For each part of this causal chain that is understood, there are doubtless a hundred that are not. The important point, however, is that in describing it as best we can, there is no need, at any stage, to

introduce mental or nonphysical substances or reactions. The diffusion of sodium ions into a neuron, for instance, with the resultant flow of current, is not
perfectly understood, but no one supposes that the understanding of this
would be enhanced by reference to nonphysical or mental events, nor is it
even possible to imagine how such nonphysical events could ever bring about,
abet, or inhibit any such ion diffusion.

We know the end result of this chain of physical processes; it is the secretion
of perspiration on the hands. We know, more or less, a good many of the intermediate processes. The baffling question that now arises, however, is how
such a complex series gets *started*. The hypothalamus, we noted, is closely
connected with the cortex and subcortical parts of the brain. Presumably,
then, it is some change within these that eventuates, finally, in the secretion of
perspiration. The brain, however, is a physical object, and the only changes it
is capable of undergoing are physical changes, similar to those manifested in
any other part of the body. If, accordingly, the mind acts upon the body to produce perspiration on the hands, it is here, in the cortex or subcortical parts of
the brain, that such interaction occurs.

But how exactly are we to conceive of this action of the mind upon that por-
tion of the brain? Presumably, thoughts — that is, ideas or images — occur
"within the mind." This must not for a moment be thought to mean that these
occur within the brain or any part of it, for they are, according to the view we
have been considering, strictly nonphysical entities having no location in
space, either within the head or elsewhere, and no physical property whatever
that would ever render them susceptible to observation or even to any detec-
tion by microscopes, probes, or any other physical apparatus. Yet these
nonphysical things do, according to this view, act upon a physical object: the
brain. What we must conceive, then, is a physical change within the brain, this
change being wrought not by some other physical change in the brain or elsewhere but by an *idea*. We do not know what that physical change in the brain
is, but that does not matter so long as it is clearly understood that it is a change
of a physical substance, the brain. We can suppose, then, just to get some sort
of picture before us, that it is a change consisting of the diffusion of sodium
ions into certain of the brain's cells. Conceive, then, if possible, how an *idea*
can effect such a change as this, how an idea can render more permeable the
membranes of certain brain cells, how an idea can enter into a chemical reac-
tion whose effect is the diffusion of sodium ions at a certain place, or how an
idea can move the particles of the cortical cells or otherwise aid or inhibit
chemical reactions occurring therein. Try, I say, to form a conception of this,
and then confess that, as soon as the smallest attempt at any description is
made, the description becomes unintelligible and the conception an impossible one. That compounds should be constituted and decomposed by physical
forces and according to physical law, that minute particles of matter should be
moved hither or thither by the action upon them of other particles, that a substance should be ionized by an electrical current or by the action of another

physical substance — all this is clearly intelligible. But that these same things should be made to happen without any physical substances or physical processes among their causal antecedents, that they should be wrought by something so nebulous as an idea or mental image, by something having no physical property and not even a location, by something that could never enter into the physical description of anything, or into any chemical equation, and in violation of the very physical laws and principles according to which all physical objects such as the brain and its parts operate — that anything like this should happen seems quite unintelligible. It is one thing to say that the mind acts upon the body. But it is quite another thing to give some clear instance of a bodily change and then try to imagine how the mind, or any thought or idea, could in any way be involved in any such change as that. To say that a diffusion of sodium ions was caused by an "idea" is not to give any causal explanation at all. It is, rather, to confess that the explanation of that diffusion is simply not known. One can in such terms always verbally describe human behavior or the activity of the nerves and brain and glands, interlarding the explanation here and there with references to mental or nonphysical processes; but no one can possibly understand what is thus verbally set forth, or form the least conception of how such interaction between wholly disparate realms of being is at all possible.

THE LOCUS OF INTERACTION

That has always been the main difficulty in any theory of the interaction of mind and body, and it is a difficulty that is hardly removed by such glib phrases as "anything can cause anything." Interactionism becomes quite unintelligible as soon as one endeavors to spell out, in some considerable detail, some bodily change, and then to show how mental or nonphysical processes can in any way be involved in such a change. It is not enough to say that the mind acts upon the body or that some particular mental thing, like an idea, acts upon some particular part of the body, such as the sweat glands. It is the precise *localization* of such activity that presents a great difficulty; as of course it must, since mental processes are, by the very description that is usually given of them, not localizable in the first place. It is sometimes suggested that the mind acts not simply on "the body," but on the *brain*, but this too is altogether too loose. We noted that the hypothalamus, which is so significantly involved in so many bodily changes, is connected in the most elaborate way with various parts of the entire cerebrospinal system. Now surely, the mind does not act directly upon the hypothalamus. The hypothalamus is acted upon by stimuli received from these other areas of the body. We must imagine it possible, then, to indicate exactly, in the case of any particular instance of alleged mind – body interaction, the locus of this interaction. In the example we were considering, for instance, we can hardly suppose that the entire cerebrospinal complex acts upon the hypothalamus to produce those changes that finally result in perspiration on the hands. It is surely some particular part of the brain, some fairly precise part of the cortex, perhaps, from which the hypothalamus receives its impulses. What the interactionist must be willing to say, accordingly, is that, in this particular instance of the action of the mind on the body, the mind acts on the body at that particular spot in the cortex. It must at least be thinkable that the part of the cortex involved could be designated with exactness — as being, for instance, that part which is just so far, and in just such and such a direction, from the lobe of the right ear. Now the interactionist must say that it is there, at that spot, that the mind acts upon the body in this example, causing, at just that spot, a diffusion of sodium ions into those cortical cells. And this, surely, is something that no one can really seriously maintain. If sodium ions are diffused into these particular cortical cells, the cause of this is a physical process within the brain, not a mental process within something belonging to a wholly different realm of being. This sort of difficulty, it will be noted, repeats itself, no matter how far back and into what remote corners of the cortex we trace the physical processes involved. To say at any point in the description that "the mind acts upon the body" is not to explain anything, but rather just to spare oneself the task of pursuing the description of the chain of physical processes any farther.

CHAPTER FOUR

The Mind
as a Function
of the Body

In response to difficulties of the sort we have considered, many thinkers and investigators, particularly those not trained in philosophy, have been eager to maintain that human beings or persons are physical objects having, of course, psychological powers and attributes that distinguish them from other kinds of physical objects, but that such psychological powers and attributes can be understood in terms of certain bodily functions, or even identified with these.

EPIPHENOMENALISM

Many such views amount to some version of epiphenomenalism, according to which mental entities, such as thoughts, images, ideas, and feelings, never enter as causes into any physical processes, and hence never act upon the body or any part of it, yet are sometimes, if not always, the effects of bodily processes, particularly those within the nervous system. Mind and body do not, then, on this view *interact*, for no mental state or event ever causes any bodily one. Yet the body does act upon the "mind" in this sense, that some, if not all, psychological states or events are the direct or indirect effects of occurrences within the body, especially those within the brain and nerves.

If, then, we ask our original question, concerning what a person essentially is, the answer turns out on this view to be something like this: A person is a living physical body having a mind, the mind consisting, however, of nothing but a more or less continuous series of conscious or unconscious states and events, such as feelings, thoughts, images, and ideas, which are the effects but never the causes of bodily activity.

Such a view does indeed avoid the apparent absurdities of ordinary interactionism, but it involves additional difficulties no less appalling and, when clearly conceived, appears so bizarre a description of human nature as to make almost any alternative conception more acceptable. For, in the first place, whatever difficulty there is in the idea of purely mental entities entering into physical chains of causation and altering, for instance, the direction and outcome of chemical reactions and mechanical processes, there is no less difficulty in the idea that purely physical chains of causation, involving chemical reactions and the like, should have effects that could in principle never enter into the physical description of anything. That bodily processes, in other words, should have nonbodily effects is no more comprehensible than that mental processes should have nonmental effects; causation in one direction is neither more nor less difficult to comprehend than in the other.

THE ALLEGED SUPERFLUITY OF THOUGHT

To see just how odd is the conception of human behavior that results from this view, we need to note carefully just what it asserts. It asserts that all bodily processes are self-contained; that is, that no mental state or event ever enters causally into any physical process. It follows, then, that all bodily behavior is caused by bodily processes alone, and that the mind, and all states and events transpiring therein, being only incidental by-products of these physical processes, are entirely superfluous so far as the understanding and explanation of human behavior are concerned. This means that it makes no difference, so far as human behavior is concerned, whether those mental states and events exist or not, that human behavior would be just what it is without them, since they in no way influence the direction or outcome of any state, process, or motion of the body. But this seems quite impossible to believe. We can, no doubt, suppose that the behavior of certain organisms such as plants and insects is nothing but the resultant of physical or chemical processes within them, and is entirely without conscious direction, but it is impossible to believe that one's thoughts and ideas have no influence upon what one does. One can hardly suppose that one's behavior would be no different even if his mental life were quite different or even nonexistent, or that even the whole of human history, with all its wars and political upheavals, would have been just what it has been even without all those thoughts and feelings that, according to this theory, superfluously attended them. What a person does is sometimes quite obviously the more or less direct outcome of what he thinks, desires, plans, and intends. Some allegedly mental states, such as twinges of pain and the like, may indeed be the mere accompaniments and effects of bodily processes, having themselves no direct influence on bodily behavior, but it is difficult to believe that one's entire mental life is the mere accompaniment and effect of bodily processes, and that those bodily processes — *i.e.*, the whole of his observable behavior — are altogether unaffected by them.

Now it might be suggested, in response to this kind of *reductio ad absurdum* of epiphenomenalism, that causes are impossible without their effects. Because thoughts, ideas, and feelings, then, are the regular effects of bodily changes, these thoughts, ideas, and feelings could not occur without bodily changes. Hence, it might be claimed, whereas such thoughts, ideas, and feelings in no way act as causes of bodily behavior, that behavior would nevertheless be impossible without them, and it is therefore false to suggest that, on this theory, a person's behavior would be no different even in the absence of those mental phenomena.

This line of thought does not, however, properly represent the epiphenomenalist position. For according to epiphenomenalism, mental states are not the effects of observable bodily behavior but of certain states of the brain and nervous system. Observable behavior, including one's voluntary acts, is likewise the effect of those same or other states of the brain and nervous system. States of the brain and nervous system, accordingly, have two entirely different *kinds* of effects, effects in two entirely different realms, the mental and the physical. Now, so long as certain brain and nervous states occur, then on this theory the observable bodily behavior that is the consequence of them is guaranteed, whether the attendant mental effects occur or not, and these latter need not therefore be taken into account at all in the explanation of human conduct. They are, then, superfluous after all, human behavior being unaffected either by their presence or their absence. Now one can indeed say that without the mental states, those particular brain and nerve states that are their normal causes could not occur, since from the nonoccurrence of the effect we can infer the nonoccurrence of its cause. But from this we cannot conclude that those mental states are necessary for the occurrence of the observable behavior of people, for that behavior might well be the effect of other bodily states, including, of course, other states of the brain and nervous system, and must in any case be the effect of *some* state of the body, according to the epiphenomenalist view.

MATERIALISM AGAIN

We have drawn no closer to an answer to our question but have, on the contrary, gotten progressively farther from it, each difficulty raising a new theory having more difficulties in it than the last. Perhaps the only sure conclusion we can draw is that human nature is mysterious. But this, however unsatisfactory, is nonetheless worth affirming, for certainly no one can hold any of the views we have outlined, or any of the numberless variations on them, entirely without embarrassment, unless one simply resolves to see no obstacles where they are nonetheless securely lodged.

One thing should by now seem quite plain, however, and that is that the difficulties of simple materialism are not overcome by any form of dualism. There is, therefore, no point in recommending dualism as an improvement over materialism. To assert that a person is both body *and* mind — that is, two things rather than one — not only does not remove any problem involved in saying that he is one thing only, namely, a body, but also introduces all the problems of describing the connection between those two things. We are led to conclude, then, that a metaphysical understanding of human nature must be sought within the framework of materialism, according to which a person is entirely identical with his body.

All forms of dualism arise from the alleged disparity between persons and physical objects. People, it is rightly noted, are capable of thinking, believing, feeling, wishing, and so on, but bodies, it is claimed, are capable of none of these things, and the conclusion is drawn that people are not bodies. Yet it cannot be denied that they *have* bodies; hence, it is decided that a person is a nonphysical entity, somehow more or less intimately related to a body. But here it is rarely noted that whatever difficulties there may be in applying personal and psychological predicates and descriptions to bodies, precisely the same difficulties are involved in applying such predicates and descriptions to *anything whatever,* including spirits or souls. If, for example, a philosopher reasons that a body cannot think and thereby affirms that, since a person thinks, a person is a soul or spirit or mind rather than a body, we are entitled to ask how a spirit can think. For surely if a spirit or soul can think, we can affirm that a body can do so; and if we are asked *how* a body can think, our reply can be that it thinks in precisely the manner in which the dualist supposes a soul thinks. The difficulty of imagining how a body thinks is not in the least lessened by asserting that something else, which is not a body, thinks. And so it is with every other personal predicate or description. Whenever faced with the dualist's challenge to explain how a body can have desires, wishes, how it can deliberate, choose, repent, how it can be intelligent or stupid, virtuous or wicked, and so on, our reply can always be: The body can do these things, and be these things, in whatever manner one imagines the soul can do these things and be these things. For to repeat, the difficulty here is in seeing how *anything at all* can deliberate, choose, repent, think, be virtuous or wicked, and so on, and *that* difficulty is not removed but simply glossed over by the invention of some new thing, henceforth to be called the "mind" or "soul."

It becomes quite obvious what is the source of dualistic metaphysics when the dualist or soul philosopher is pressed for some description of the mind or soul. The mind or soul, it turns out in such descriptions, is just whatever it is that thinks, reasons, deliberates, chooses, feels, and so on. But the fact with which we began was that *human beings* think, reason, deliberate, choose, feel, and so on. And we do in fact have some fairly clear notion of what we mean by a human being, for we think of an individual person as existing in space and time, having a certain height and weight — as a being, in short, having many things in common with other objects in space and time, and particularly with those that are living, *i.e.*, with other animals. But the dualist, noting that a human being is significantly different from other beings, insofar as he, unlike most of them, is capable of thinking, deliberating, choosing, and so on, suddenly asserts that it is not a person, as previously conceived, that does these things at all, but something else, namely, a mind or soul, or something that does not exist in space and time nor have any height and weight, nor have, in fact, any material properties at all. And then when we seek some understanding of what this mind or soul is, we find it simply described as a thing that thinks, deliberates, feels, and so on. But surely the proper inference should have been that people are like all other physical objects in some respects — *e.g.*, in having size, mass, and location in space and time; that they are like some physical objects but unlike others in certain further respects — *e.g.*, in being living, sentient, and so on; and like no other physical objects at all in still other respects — *e.g.*, in being rational, deliberative, and so on. And of course none of this suggests that people are not physical objects, but rather that they are precisely physical objects, like other bodies in some ways, unlike many other bodies in other ways, and unlike any other bodies in still other respects.

The dualist or soul philosopher reasons that since people think, feel, desire, choose, and so on, and since such things cannot be asserted of bodies, then people are not bodies. Reasoning in this fashion, we are forced to the conclusion that people are not bodies — though it is a stubborn fact that they nevertheless *have* bodies. So the great problem then is to connect people, now conceived as souls or minds, to their bodies. But philosophically, it is just exactly as good to reason that, since people think, feel, desire, choose, etc., and since people are bodies — *i.e.*, are living animal organisms having the essential material attributes of weight, size, and so on — then *some* bodies think, feel, desire, choose, etc. This argument is just as good as the dualist's argument and does not lead us into a morass of problems concerning the connection between soul and body.

THE SOURCE OF DUALISTIC THEORIES

Why, then, does the dualist's argument have, and this argument lack, such an initial plausibility? Why have so many philosophers been led into dualistic metaphysical views, on the basis of arguments apparently no stronger than other arguments having simpler conclusions but that are rarely even considered?

Part of the answer is perhaps that, when we form an idea of a *body* or a *physical object*, what is most likely to come to mind is not some person or animal but something much simpler, such as a stone or a marble. When we are then invited to consider whether a physical object might think, deliberate, choose, and the like, we are led to contemplate the evident absurdity of supposing things like *that* do such things, and thus we readily receive the claim that bodies cannot think, deliberate, choose, and the like; and the dualist extracts his conclusion. But suppose we began somewhat differently. Suppose we began with a consideration of two quite dissimilar physical objects — a living animal body, of the kind commonly denominated "person," on the one hand, and a simple body, of the kind denominated "stone," on the other. Now let it be asked whether there is any absurdity in supposing that one of these things might be capable of thinking, deliberating, choosing, and the like. Here there is no absurdity at all in asserting that an object of the first kind might indeed have such capacities, but evidently not one of the second kind — from which we would conclude, not that people are not physical objects, but rather that they are physical objects that are significantly different from other physical objects, such as stones. And there is of course nothing the least astonishing in this.

But how, one may wonder, can a "mere physical object" have feelings? But here the answer should be: Why, if it is a physical object of a certain familiar kind, should it not have feelings? Suppose, for example, that it is a living body, like a frog or mouse, equipped with a complicated and living nervous system. Where is the absurdity in asserting that a "mere physical object" of this sort can feel? Evidently there is none. Hardly anyone would want to insist that beings of this sort — frogs and mice, for instance — must have souls to enable them to feel. It seems enough that they have complicated living nervous systems.

The same type of answer can be given if it is asked how a "mere physical object" can think. If we suppose that it is a physical object of a certain familiar kind, namely, a living body having the form and other visible attributes of a person, and possessed of an enormously complex living brain and nervous system — in short, that the object in question is a living human being — then there is no absurdity in supposing that this being thinks. Any argument purporting to show that such a being cannot think and must therefore have a nonmaterial soul to do its thinking for it would be just as good an argument to show that frogs and mice cannot feel, and must therefore have souls to do their feeling for them. The outcome of such philosophizing is just as good, and just as absurd, in the one case as it is in the other.

Now the materialist would, of course, like to maintain that psychological states, such as feeling, believing, desiring, and so on, are really nothing but perfectly *familiar kinds* of material states, that is, states of the body, particularly of the brain and nervous system; states that are either observable or testable by the usual methods of biology, physics, and chemistry. But this, as we have seen earlier, seems to be a vain hope, and it will always be an obstacle to any simple materialism. There is always, it seems, something that can be asserted of certain psychological states that makes little if any sense when asserted of any ordinary or familiar state of matter. One can say of a belief, for instance, that it is true or false, but this can never be said, except metaphorically or derivatively, of any familiar state of matter, such as an arrangement of molecules; we could say of such a thing that it is true or false, only if we first assumed that it is identical with some belief that is such. Again, one can say of a desire that it is the desire *for* this or that — for instance, the desire for food; of a fear that it is a fear *of* something — for instance, a fear of heights; but of no familiar state of matter can it be said that it is, in the same sense, *for* or *of* anything. It just *is* the state of matter that it is. Suppose, for example, that the materialist should say that the feeling of hunger is simply *identical* with a certain familiar state of the body, not merely that it is prompted by that state but that it *is* that state and is describable in terms of the concepts of physics and chemistry. Thus, let us suppose him to claim that hunger just *is* the state consisting of having an empty stomach, together with a deficiency of certain salts or other substances in the blood, and a certain physical disequilibrium of the nervous system consequent upon these conditions. Now there is, of course, no doubt an intimate connection between such states as these and the desire for food, but the assertion of their *identity* with that desire will always be plagued because, unlike the desire, those bodily states can be fully described without mentioning food at all, and without saying that they are in any sense states that are *for* food. Indeed, the notion of something being *for* or *of* something else, in the sense in which a desire may be a desire *for* food, or a fear may be a fear *of* heights, is not a concept of physics or chemistry at all. And yet it can surely be said of a certain desire that it is a desire for food, or of a certain fear that it is a fear of heights. The referential character of such states seems, indeed, essential to any proper description of them. Significantly, when those substances that are physiologically associated with such states are artificially administered to someone, in the effort to create within him those states themselves, the effort fails. It is fairly well known, for example, what physiological changes a person undergoes when in a state of fear; but when these changes are artificially evoked, the person does not experience fear in the usual sense. He describes his state as being vaguely *like* fear but finds that he is not afraid *of* anything.

But although psychological states are thus evidently not identical with any familiar bodily states, it does not follow that they are identical with no state of matter at all. They may, in fact, be unfamiliar states of matter, that is, states of the body that are not observable or testable by the ordinary methods of biology, physics, and chemistry. This suggestion is not as question-begging as it appears, for it is conceded by the most resolute soul philosophers and dualists that psychological states are strange ones in this respect, and that, at the very least, they are not thus observable. From the fact that some state is unobservable by the usual methods of scientific observation, nothing whatever follows with respect to the truth or falseness of materialism. From the fact that a certain state is in some respect unusual it does not follow that it is a state of an unusual thing, of a soul rather than a body, but rather, that if it is a state of the body it is an unusual one, and if it is a state of the soul it is no less unusual. Nothing is made clearer, more comprehensible, or less strange by postulating some new substance as the subject of certain states not familiar to the natural sciences, and then baptizing that new substance "the mind" or "the soul." Nor does one avoid materialism at this point by saying that by the "mind" or "soul" we just *mean* that which is the subject of psychological states; for while that might indeed be true, it is nevertheless an open question whether what we thus mean by the "mind" or "soul" might not turn out, after all, to be what we ordinarily denominate "the body." The existence of nothing whatever can be derived from any definitions of terms.

THE SOUL

This point can perhaps be borne home to the imagination by the following sort of consideration: Suppose one feels, as probably everyone more or less does, that a *person* cannot be a mere *body*, and that no increase in the physical, biological, and physiological complexity of any body can bridge the gulf between being a body, albeit a complicated and living one, and being a person. Consider, then, a highly complex and living animal organism, physically and biologically identical in every respect to a living man, but lacking that one thing that is, we are supposing, still needed in order to convert this body into a person. Now just what can this extra essential ingredient be? What do we need to *add* to convert a mere body into a person?

Let us suppose it is a *soul*. If we add a soul to this living, complicated animal organism, let us suppose, then *lo!* it will cease to be a mere body and become a person. No one knows, however, exactly what a soul is or what properties it must possess in order to confer personality upon something. All we can say is that it is what distinguishes a person from a mere body, which of course tells us nothing here. So let us give it some definite properties. It does not matter what properties we give it, as we shall shortly see, so to make it simple and easy to grasp, let us suppose that this soul is a small round ball, about the size of a marble, transparent and indestructible. Now clearly, by implanting *that* anywhere in the living organism we get no closer to converting it from a mere body to a person. We manage only to add one further, trivial complication. But why so? Why are we now no closer to having a person than before? Is it just because the "soul" we added is itself a mere body? If that is the difficulty, then let us remove its corporeality. Let us suppose that the soul we add to this living animal organism is not a small round *physical* ball but a nonphysical one. This will permit us to retain its transparency. If, being nonphysical, it can no longer be described as a ball, then we can drop that part of the description too. Let the thing we add be, in short, anything one likes. Let it be a small hard ball, a small soft ball, an immaterial ball, or something that is neither material nor a ball. The point is that no matter *what* it is that is added, it goes not the least way toward converting what was a mere body into a person. If a small hard ball does not bridge the gap, then we get no closer to bridging it by simply removing its properties of hardness, smallness, and sphericity — by making it, in short, something that is merely *non*physical. What we need to do is state just what positive properties this extra thing must possess, in order to elevate an animal body to the status of a person, and no positive properties suggest themselves at all. We cannot give it psychological properties — by saying, for example, that this soul thinks, desires, deliberates, wills, believes, repents, and so on; for if the thing we are adding has *those* properties, then it is *already* a person in its own right, and there is no question of *adding* it to something in order to get a person. We could as easily have given *those* properties to the animal organism with which we began as to give them to something else and then super-fluously amalgamate the two things. Plainly, there are no positive properties of any "soul" that will do the trick. The best we can do is to say that the extra something required — the soul, or the mind, or whatever we choose to call this additional thing — is that which, when added, makes up the difference be-tween being a mere animal body and being a person. This is about as good a way as one could find for indicating that he has no idea what he is talking about.

THE "PRIVACY" OF PSYCHOLOGICAL STATES

One final point will serve to illustrate the futility of dualistic hypotheses as so-lutions to difficulties admittedly inherent in any materialistic theory.

The states of the mind or soul, it is said, are simply those states that are not observable by any ordinary way but that can nevertheless be known, by an immediate awareness, to the person who has them. It is thus the *privacy* of such states that marks them as mental and, being mental, it is forthwith con-cluded that they are states of a mind or soul rather than of a body, and some-times that the person who is aware of them is identical with that mind or soul. But concerning some such states — namely, pains and other simple sensa-tions, which are most assuredly private — there is an absurdity in asserting that they are states of the mind or soul.

Suppose, for instance, that one has a decayed tooth or a lacerated toe. Now the dentist, it is said, can observe, perhaps in minute detail, the condition of the tooth, and the physician the condition of the toe, but neither can have any awareness of the pain associated with either, pains that are nevertheless felt by that person whose tooth or toe is thus damaged. The conclusion is then drawn that the dentist and physician are aware only of states of the body, while the patient is aware of something else that, being no state of the body, must be a state of the mind or soul.

But surely all that follows from such an argument is that persons other than oneself can observe some, but not others, of one's states. It does not at all follow that those private states — pains, in this case — are states of some further thing, such as a mind or soul, that is unobservable. From the fact that some state is, in the sense described, private, it does not follow that it is a state of a private thing. The argument is, in short, a simple *non sequitur.*

The conclusion of the argument is moreover absurd; for that conclusion is that a toothache or a toe ache is a state of mind, or a condition of the soul, which it manifestly is not. A toothache is a state of the tooth, and a toe ache a state of the toe. That the dentist and physician cannot observe these states does not show that they are states of the mind or soul rather than of the tooth and toe, but only that some of a person's states are not observable to dentists and doctors, which is hardly surprising. The physician, contemplating one's lacerated toe, might reasonably ask whether *it* hurts, and in doing so he would be inquiring about the toe and nothing else. The pain that the patient feels, moreover, is felt in the toe. It would be an utter distortion to say that the pain is felt in, or by, the mind, and then somehow *referred* to the toe. And it would be not only a distortion but an absurdity for the patient to say that he feels pain in his mind, or that a pain is felt by his mind, this pain being occasioned by a condition of his toe. The pain is located, by the patient, in his toe, just as surely as the wound; that is where the pain is felt, nowhere else. What the patient can truly say is that *he* feels pain and that the pain he feels is in his toe. In thus referring to himself as the subject of the feeling, he is not referring to some metaphysical thing, like a soul or mind, and saying that *it* feels pain; he is referring to himself, as a person — that is, as a living animal organism, seated here and now before the physician, an animal organism with which he identifies himself, and saying that this person, himself, feels pain. And the pain that he feels, he surely does not doubt, is in his toe. At no point in his discussion with the physician could it ever be relevant in this situation to make any reference to his mind or his soul; it is not the soul or mind that hurts but the toe, nor is it the soul or mind that feels it, but he himself, the very person, the very animal organism, the very living, physical body that is sitting there.

Of course we cannot, by these reflections, pretend to have solved the problems of mind and matter, nor to have proved any theory of materialism. Human nature is mysterious, and remains so, no matter what one's metaphysical theory is or how simple it is. It does nevertheless seem evident that no dualistic theory of man renders human nature any less mysterious, and that whatever questions are left unanswered by the materialist are left equally unanswered, though perhaps better concealed, by his opponents.

CHAPTER FIVE

Freedom and Determinism

If I consider the world or any part of it at any particular moment, it seems certain that it is perfectly determinate in every detail. There is no vagueness, looseness, or ambiguity. There is, indeed, vagueness, and even error, in my conceptions of reality, but not in reality itself. A lilac bush, which surely has a certain exact number of blossoms, appears to me only to have many blossoms, and I do not know how many. Things seen in the distance appear of indefinite form, and often of a color and size that in fact they are not. Things near the border of my visual field seem to me vague and amorphous, and I can never even say exactly where that border itself is, it is so indefinite and vague. But all such indeterminateness resides solely in my conceptions and ideas; the world itself shares none of it. The sea, at any exact time and place, has exactly a certain salinity and temperature, and every grain of sand on its shore is exactly disposed with respect to all the others. The wind at any point in space has at any moment a certain direction and force, not more nor less. It matters not whether these properties and relations are known to anyone. A field of wheat at any moment contains just an exact number of ripening grains, each having reached just the ripeness it exhibits, each presenting a determinate color and shade, an exact shape and mass. A person, too, at any given point in his life, is perfectly determinate to the minutest cells of his body. My own brain, nerves — even my thoughts, intentions, and feelings — are at any moment just what they then specifically are. These thoughts might, to be sure, be vague and even false as representations, but as thoughts they are not, and even a false idea is no less an exact and determinate idea than a true one.

Nothing seems more obvious. But if I now ask *why* the world and all its larger or smaller parts are this moment just what they are, the answer comes to mind: because the world, the moment before, was precisely what it then was. Given exactly what went before, the world, it seems, could now be none other than it is. And what it was a moment before, in all its larger and minuter parts, was the consequence of what had gone just before then, and so on, back to the very beginning of the world, if it had a beginning, or through an infinite past time, in case it had not. In any case, the world as it now is, and every part of it, and every detail of every part, would seem to be the only world that now could be, given just what it has been.

DETERMINISM

Reflections such as this suggest that, in the case of everything that exists, there are antecedent conditions, known or unknown, which, because they are given, mean that things could not be other than they are. That is an exact statement of the metaphysical thesis of determinism. More loosely, it says that everything, including every cause, is the effect of some cause or causes; or that everything is not only determinate but causally determined. The statement, moreover, makes no allowance for time, for past, or for future. Hence, if true, it holds not only for all things that have existed but for all things that do or ever will exist.

Of course people rarely think of such a principle, and hardly one in a thousand will ever formulate it to himself in words. Yet all do seem to assume it in their daily affairs, so much so that some philosophers have declared it an *a priori* principle of the understanding, that is, something that is known independently of experience, while others have deemed it to be at least a part of the common sense of mankind. Thus, when I hear a noise I look up to see where it came from. I never suppose that it was just a noise that came from nowhere and had no cause. Everyone does the same — even animals, though they have never once thought about metaphysics or the principle of universal determinism. People believe, or at least act as though they believed, that things have causes, without exception. When a child or animal touches a hot stove for the first time, it unhesitatingly believes that the pain then felt was caused by that stove, and so firm and immediate is that belief that hot stoves are avoided ever after. We all use our metaphysical principles, whether we think of them or not, or are even capable of thinking of them. If I have a bodily or other disorder — a rash, for instance, or a fever or a phobia — I consult a physician for a diagnosis and explanation in the hope that the cause of it might be found and removed or moderated. I am never tempted to suppose that such things just have no causes, arising from nowhere, else I would take no steps to remove the causes. The principle of determinism is here, as in everything else, simply assumed, without being thought about.

DETERMINISM AND HUMAN BEHAVIOR

I am a part of the world. So is each of the cells and minute parts of which I am composed. The principle of determinism, then, in case it is true, applies to me and to each of those minute parts, no less than to the sand, wheat, winds, and waters of which we have spoken. There is no particular difficulty in thinking so, as long as I consider only what are sometimes called the "purely physiological" changes of my body, like growth, the pulse, glandular secretions, and the like. But what of my thoughts and ideas? And what of my behavior that is supposed to be deliberate, purposeful, and perhaps morally significant? These are all changes of my own being, changes that I undergo, and if these are all but the consequences of the conditions under which they occur, and these conditions are the only ones that could have obtained, given the state of the world just before and when they arose, what now becomes of my responsibility for my behavior and of the control over my conduct that I fancy myself to possess? What am I but a helpless product of nature, destined by her to do whatever I do and to become whatever I become?

There is no moral blame nor merit in anyone who cannot help what he does. It matters not whether the explanation for his behavior is found within him or without, whether it is expressed in terms of ordinary physical causes or allegedly "mental" ones, or whether the causes be proximate or remote. I am not responsible for being a man rather than a woman, nor for having the temperament and desires characteristic of that sex. I was never asked whether these should be given to me. The kleptomaniac, similarly, steals from compulsion, the alcoholic drinks from compulsion, and sometimes even the hero dies from compulsive courage. Though these causes are within them, they compel no less for that, and their victims never chose to have them inflicted upon themselves. To say they are compulsions is to say only that they compel. But to say that they compel is only to say that they cause; for the cause of a thing being given, the effect cannot fail to follow. By the thesis of determinism, however, everything whatever is caused, and not one single thing could ever be other than exactly what it is. Perhaps one thinks that the kleptomaniac and the drunkard did not have to become what they are, that they could have done better at another time and thereby ended up better than they are now, or that the hero could have done worse and then ended up a coward. But this shows only an unwillingness to understand what made them become as they are. Having found that their behavior is caused from within them, we can hardly avoid asking what caused these inner springs of action, and then asking what were the causes of these causes, and so on through the infinite past. We shall not, certainly, with our small understanding and our fragmentary knowledge of the past ever know why the world should at just this time and place have produced just this thief, this drunkard, and this hero, but the vagueness and smattered nature of our knowledge should not tempt us to imagine a similar vagueness in nature herself. Everything in nature is and always has been determinate, with no loose edges at all, and she was forever destined to bring forth just what she has produced, however slight may be our understanding of the origins of these works. Ultimate responsibility for anything that exists, and hence for any person and his deeds, can thus rest only with the first cause of all things, if there is such a cause, or nowhere at all, in case there is not. Such, at least, seems to be the unavoidable implication of determinism.

DETERMINISM AND MORALS

Some philosophers, faced with all this, which seems quite clear to the ordinary understanding, have tried to cling to determinism while modifying traditional conceptions of morals. They continue to *use* such words as *merit, blame, praise,* and *desert,* but they so divest them of their meanings as to finish by talking about things entirely different, sometimes without themselves realizing that they are no longer on the subject. An ordinary person will hardly understand that anyone can possess merit or vice and be deserving of moral praise or blame, as a result of traits that he has or of behavior arising from those traits, once it is well understood that he could never have avoided being just what he is and doing just what he does.

We are happily spared going into all this, however, for the question whether determinism is true of human nature is not a question of ethics at all but of metaphysics. There is accordingly no hope of answering it within the context of ethics. One can, to be sure, simply *assume* an answer to it — assume that determinism is true, for instance — and then see what are the implications of this answer for ethics; but that does not answer the question. Or one can *assume* some theory or other of ethics — assume some version of "the greatest happiness" principle, for instance — and then see whether that theory is consistent with determinism. But such confrontations of theories with theories likewise make us no wiser, so far as any fundamental question is concerned. We can suppose at once that determinism is consistent with some conceptions of morals, and inconsistent with others, and that the same holds for indeterminism. We shall still not know what theories are true; we shall only know which are consistent with another.

We shall, then, eschew all considerations of ethics as having no real bearing on our problem. We want to learn, if we can, whether determinism is true, and this is a question of metaphysics. It can, like all good questions of philosophy, be answered only on the basis of certain data; that is, by seeing whether or not it squares with certain things that everyone knows, or believes himself to know, or with things everyone is at least more sure about than the answer to the question at issue.

Now I could, of course, simply affirm that I am a morally responsible being, in the sense in which my responsibility for my behavior implies that I could have avoided that behavior. But this would take us into the nebulous realm of ethics, and it is, in fact, far from obvious that I am responsible in that sense. Many have doubted that they are responsible in that sense, and it is in any case not difficult to doubt it, however strongly one might feel about it.

There are, however, two things about myself of which I feel quite certain and that have no necessary connection with morals. The first is that I sometimes deliberate, with the view to making a decision; a decision, namely, to do this thing or that. And the second is that whether or not I deliberate about what to do, it is sometimes up to me what I do. This might all be an illusion, of course; but so also might any philosophical theory, such as the theory of determinism, be false. The point remains that it is far more difficult for me to doubt that I sometimes deliberate, and that it is sometimes up to me what to do, than to doubt any philosophical theory whatever, including the theory of determinism. We must, accordingly, if we ever hope to be wiser, adjust our theories to our data and not try to adjust our data to our theories.

Let us, then, get these two data quite clearly before us so we can see what they are, what they presuppose, and what they do and do not entail.

DELIBERATION

Deliberation is an activity, or at least a kind of experience, that cannot be defined, or even described, without metaphors. We speak of weighing this and that in our minds, of trying to anticipate consequences of various possible courses of action, and so on, but such descriptions do not convey to us what deliberation is unless we already know.

Whenever I deliberate, however, I find that I make certain presuppositions, whether I actually think of them or not. That is, I assume that certain things are true, certain things which are such that, if I thought they were not true, it would be impossible for me to deliberate at all. Some of these can be listed as follows:

First, I find that I can deliberate only about my own behavior and never about the behavior of another. I can try to guess, speculate, or figure out what another person is going to do; I can read certain signs and sometimes infer what he will do; but I cannot deliberate about it. When I deliberate I try to decide something, to make up my mind, and this is as remote as anything could be from speculating, trying to guess, or inferring from signs. Sometimes one *does* speculate on what he is going to do, by trying to draw conclusions from certain signs or omens — he might infer that he is going to sneeze, for instance, or speculate that he is going to become a grandfather — but he is not then deliberating whether to do things or not. One does, to be sure, sometimes deliberate about whether another person will do a certain act, when that other person is subject to his command or otherwise under his control; but then he is not really deliberating about another person's acts at all, but about his own — namely, whether or not to have that other person carry out the order.

Second, I find that I can deliberate only about future things, never things past or present. I may not know what I did at a certain time in the past, in case I have forgotten, but I can no longer deliberate whether to do it then or not. I can, again, only speculate, guess, try to infer, or perhaps try to remember. Similarly, I cannot deliberate whether or not to be doing something now; I can only ascertain whether or not I am in fact doing it. If I am sitting I cannot deliberate about whether or not to be sitting. I can only deliberate about whether to remain sitting — and this has to do with the future.

Third, I cannot deliberate about what I shall do if I already know what I am going to do. If I were to say, for example, "I know that I am going to be married tomorrow and in the meantime I am going to deliberate about whether to get married," I would contradict myself. There are only two ways that I could know now what I am going to do tomorrow; namely, either by inferring this from certain signs and omens or by having already decided what I am going to do. But if I have inferred from signs and omens what I am going to do, I cannot deliberate about it — there is just nothing for me to decide; and similarly, if I have already decided. If, on the other hand, I can still deliberate about what I am going to do, to that extent I must regard the signs and omens as unreliable, and the inference uncertain, and I therefore do not know what I am going to do after all.

And finally, I cannot deliberate about what to do, even though I may not know what I am going to do, unless I believe that it is up to me what I am going to do. If I am within the power of another person, or at the mercy of circumstances over which I have no control, then, although I may have no idea what I am going to do, I cannot deliberate about it. I can only wait and see. If, for instance, I am a serviceman, and regulations regarding uniforms are posted each day by my commanding officer and are strictly enforced by him, then I shall not know what uniforms I shall be wearing from time to time, but I cannot deliberate about it. I can only wait and see what regulations are posted; it is not up to me. Similarly, a woman who is about to give birth to a child cannot deliberate whether to have a boy or a girl, even though she may not know. She can only wait and see; it is not up to her. Such examples can be generalized to cover any case wherein one does not know what he is going to do but believes that it is not up to him, and hence no matter for his decision and hence none for his deliberation.

"IT IS UP TO ME"

I sometimes feel certain that it is, at least to some extent, up to me what I am going to do; indeed, I must believe this if I am to deliberate about what to do. But what does this mean? It is, again, hard to say, but the idea can be illustrated, and we can fairly easily see what it does *not* mean.

Let us consider the simplest possible sort of situation in which this belief might be involved. At this moment, for instance, it seems quite certain to me that, holding my finger before me, I can move it either to the left or to the right, that each of these motions is possible for me. This does not mean merely that my finger can move either way, although it entails that, for this would be true in case nothing obstructed it, even if I had no control over it at all. I can say of a distant, fluttering leaf that it can move either way, but not that I can move it, since I have no control over it. How it moves is not up to me. Nor does it mean merely that my finger can be moved either way, although it entails this too. If the motions of my finger are under the control of some other person or of some machine, then it might be true that the finger can be moved either way, by that person or machine, though false that I can move it at all.

If I say, then, that it is up to me how I move my finger, I mean that I can move it in this way and I can move it in that way, and not merely that it can move or be moved in this way and that. I mean that the motion of my finger is within my direct control. If someone were to ask me to move it to the right, I could do that, and if he were to ask me to move it to the left, I could do that too. Further, I could do these simple acts without being asked at all, and having been asked, I could move it in a manner the exact opposite of what was requested, since I can ignore the request. There are, to be sure, some motions of my finger that I cannot make, so it is not *entirely* up to me how it moves. I cannot bend it backward, for instance, or bend it into a knot, for these motions are obstructed by the very anatomical construction of the finger itself; and to say that I can move my finger at all means at least that nothing obstructs such a motion, though it does not mean merely this. There is, however, at this moment, no obstruction, anatomical or otherwise, to my moving it to the right, and none to my moving it to the left.

This datum, it should be noted, is properly expressed as a conjunction and not as a disjunction. That is, my belief is that I can move my finger in one way *and* that I can also move it another way; and it does not do justice to this belief to say that I can move it one way *or* the other. It is fairly easy to see the truth of this, for the latter claim, that I can move it one way *or* the other, would be satisfied in case there were only one way I could move it, and *that* is not what I believe. Suppose, for instance, that my hand were strapped to a device in such a fashion that I could move my finger to the right but not to the left. Then it would still be entirely true that I could move it either to the left *or* to the right — since it would be true that I could move it to the right. But that is not what I now believe. My finger is not strapped to anything, and nothing obstructs its motion in either direction. And what I believe, in this situation, is that I can move it to the right *and* I can move it to the left.

We must note further that the belief expressed in our datum is not a belief in what is logically impossible. It is the belief that I now *can* move my finger in different ways but not that I can move it in different ways at once. What I believe is that I am now able to move my finger one way and that I am now equally able to move it another way, but I do not claim to be able now or at any other time to move it both ways simultaneously. The situation here is analogous to one in which I might, for instance, be offered a choice of either of two apples but forbidden to take both. Each apple is such that I may select it, but neither is such that I may select it together with the other.

Now, are these two data — the belief that I do sometimes deliberate, and the belief that it is sometimes up to me what I do — consistent with the metaphysical theory of determinism? We do not know yet. We intend to find out. It is fairly clear, however, that they are going to present difficulties to that theory. But let us not, in any case, try to avoid those difficulties by just denying the data themselves. If we eventually deny the data, we shall do so for better reasons than this. Virtually everyone is convinced that beliefs such as are expressed in our data are sometimes true. They cannot be simply dismissed as false just because they might appear to conflict with a metaphysical theory that hardly anyone has ever really thought much about at all. Almost anyone, unless his fingers are paralyzed, bound, or otherwise incapable of movement, believes sometimes that the motions of his fingers are within his control, in exactly the sense expressed by our data. If consequences of considerable importance to him depend on how he moves his fingers, he sometimes deliberates before moving them, or at least he is convinced that he does or that he can. Philosophers might have different notions of just what things are implied by such data, but there is in any case no more, and in fact considerably less, reason for denying the data than for denying some philosophical theory.

CAUSAL VERSUS LOGICAL NECESSITY

Philosophers have long since pointed out that causal connections involve no logical necessity, that the denial of a particular causal connection is never self-contradictory, and this is undoubtedly true. But neither does the assertion or the denial of determinism involve any concept of what is and what is not logically necessary. If determinism is true, then anything that happens is, given the conditions under which it occurs, the only thing possible, the thing that is necessitated by those conditions. But it is not the only thing that is logically possible, nor do those conditions logically necessitate it. Similarly, if one denies the thesis of determinism by asserting, for instance, that each of two bodily motions is possible for him under identical conditions, he is asserting much more than that each is logically possible, for that would be a trivial claim.

This distinction, between logical necessity and the sort of necessity involved in determinism, can be illustrated with examples. If, for instance, a man is beheaded, we can surely say that it is impossible for him to go on living, that his being beheaded necessitates his death, and so on; but there are no logical necessities or impossibilities involved here. It is not logically impossible for a man to live without his head. Yet no one will deny that a man cannot live under conditions that include his being headless, that such a state of affairs is in a perfectly clear sense impossible. Similarly, if my finger is in a tight and fairly strong cast, then it is impossible for me to move it in any way at all, though this is not logically impossible. It is logically possible that I should be vastly stronger than I am, and that I should move my finger and, in doing so, break the cast, though this would ordinarily not be possible in the sense that concerns us. Again, it is not logically impossible that I should bend my finger backward, or into a knot, though it is, in fact, impossible for me to do either or, what means the same thing, necessary that I should do neither. Certain conditions prohibit my doing such things, though they impose no logical barrier. And finally, if someone — a physician, for example — should ask me whether I can move my finger, and I should reply truthfully that I can, I would not merely be telling her that it is logically possible for me to move it, for this she already knows. I would be telling her that I am able to move it, that it is within my power to do so, that there are no conditions, such as paralysis or whatnot, that prevent my moving it.

It follows that not all necessity is logical necessity, nor all impossibility logical impossibility, and that to say that something is possible is sometimes to say much more than that it is logically possible. The kind of necessity involved in the thesis of determinism is quite obviously the nonlogical kind, as is also the kind of possibility involved in its denial. If we needed a *name* for these nonlogical modalities, we could call them *causal* necessity, impossibility, and possibility, but the concepts are clear enough without making a great deal of the name.

FREEDOM

To say that it is, in a given instance, up to me what I do is to say that I am in that instance *free* with respect to what I then do. Thus, I am sometimes free to move my finger this way and that, but not, certainly, to bend it backward or into a knot. But what does this mean?

It means, first that there is no *obstacle* or *impediment* to my activity. Thus, there is sometimes no obstacle to my moving my finger this way and that, though there are obvious obstacles to my moving it backward or into a knot. Those things, accordingly, that pose obstacles to my motions limit my freedom. If my hand were strapped in such a way as to permit only a leftward motion of my finger, I would not then be free to move it to the right. If it were encased in a tight cast that permitted no motion, I would not be free to move it at all. Freedom of motion, then, is limited by obstacles.

Further, to say that it is, in a given instance, up to me what I do, means that nothing *constrains* or *forces* me to do one thing rather than another. Constraints are like obstacles, except that while the latter prevent, the former enforce. Thus, if my finger is being forcibly bent to the left — by a machine, for instance, or by another person, or by any force that I cannot overcome — then

I am not free to move it this way and that. I cannot, in fact, move it at all; I can only watch to see how it is moved, and perhaps vainly resist: Its motions are not up to me, or within my control, but in the control of some other thing or person.

Obstacles and constraints, then, both obviously limit my freedom. To say that I am free to perform some action thus means at least that there is no obstacle to my doing it, and that nothing constrains me to do otherwise.

Now if we rest content with this observation, as many have, and construe free activity simply as activity that is unimpeded and unconstrained, there is evidently no inconsistency between affirming both the thesis of determinism and the claim that I am sometimes free. For to say that some action of mine is neither impeded nor constrained does not by itself imply that it is not causally determined. The absence of obstacles and constraints is a mere negative condition, and does not by itself rule out the presence of positive causes. It might seem, then, that we can say of some of my actions that there are conditions antecedent to their performance so that no other actions were possible, and also that these actions were unobstructed and unconstrained. And to say that would logically entail that such actions were both causally determined, and free.

SOFT DETERMINISM

It is this kind of consideration that has led many philosophers to embrace what is sometimes called "soft determinism." All versions of this theory have in common three claims, by means of which, it is naïvely supposed, a reconciliation is achieved between determinism and freedom. Freedom being, furthermore, a condition of moral responsibility and the only condition that metaphysics seriously questions, it is supposed by the partisans of this view that determinism is perfectly compatible with such responsibility. This, no doubt, accounts for its great appeal and wide acceptance, even by some people of considerable learning.

The three claims of soft determinism are (1) that the thesis of determinism is true, and that accordingly all human behavior, voluntary or other, like the behavior of all other things, arises from antecedent conditions, given which no other behavior is possible — in short, that all human behavior is caused and determined; (2) that voluntary behavior is nonetheless free to the extent that it is not externally constrained or impeded; and (3) that, in the absence of such obstacles and constraints, the causes of voluntary behavior are certain states, events, or conditions within the agent himself; namely, his own acts of will or volitions, choices, decisions, desires, and so on.

Thus, on this view, I am free, and therefore sometimes responsible for what I do, provided nothing prevents me from acting according to my own choice, desire, or volition, or constrains me to act otherwise. There may, to be sure, be other conditions for my responsibility — such as, for example, an understanding of the probable consequences of my behavior, and that sort of thing — but absence of constraint or impediment is, at least, one such condition. And, it is claimed, it is a condition that is compatible with the supposition that my behavior is caused — for it is, by hypothesis, caused by my own inner choices, desires, and volitions.

THE REFUTATION OF THIS

The theory of soft determinism looks good at first — so good that it has for generations been solemnly taught from innumerable philosophical chairs and implanted in the minds of students as sound philosophy — but no great acumen is needed to discover that far from solving any problem, it only camouflages it.

My free actions are those unimpeded and unconstrained motions that arise from my own inner desires, choices, and volitions; let us grant this provisionally. But now, whence arise those inner states that determine what my body shall do? Are they within my control or not? Having made my choice or decision and acted upon it, could I have chosen otherwise or not?

Here the determinist, hoping to surrender nothing and yet to avoid the problem implied in that question, bids us not to ask it; the question itself, he announces, is without meaning. For to say that I could have done otherwise, he says, means only that I *would* have done otherwise, *if* those inner states that determined my action had been different; if, that is, I had decided or chosen differently. To ask, accordingly, whether I could have chosen or decided differently is only to ask whether, had I decided to decide differently or chosen to choose differently, or willed to will differently, I *would* have decided or chosen or willed differently. And this, of course, *is* unintelligible nonsense.

But it is not nonsense to ask whether the causes of my actions — my own inner choices, decisions, and desires — are themselves caused. And of course they are, if determinism is true, for on that thesis everything is caused and determined. And if they are, then we cannot avoid concluding that, given the causal conditions of those inner states, I could not have decided, willed, chosen, or desired other than I, in fact, did, for this is a logical consequence of the very definition of determinism. Of course we can still say that, *if* the causes of those inner states, whatever they were, had been different, then their effects, those inner states themselves, would have been different, and that in this hypothetical sense I could have decided, chosen, willed, or desired differently — but that only pushes our problem back still another step. For we will then want to know whether the causes of those inner states were within my control, and so on *ad infinitum*. We are, at each step, permitted to say "could have been otherwise" only in a provisional sense — provided, that is, that something else had been different — but must then retract it and replace it with "could not have been otherwise" as soon as we discover, as we must at each step, that whatever would have to have been different could not have been different.

EXAMPLES

Such is the dialectic of the problem. The easiest way to see the shadowy quality of soft determinism, however, is by means of examples.

Let us suppose that my body is moving in various ways, that these motions are not externally constrained or impeded, and that they are all exactly in accordance with my own desires, choices, or acts of will and whatnot. When I will that my arm should move in a certain way, I find it moving in that way, unobstructed and unconstrained. When I will to speak, my lips and tongue move, unobstructed and unconstrained, in a manner suitable to the formation of the words I choose to utter. Now, given that this is a correct description of my behavior, namely, that it consists of the unconstrained and unimpeded motions of my body in response to my own volitions, then it follows that my behavior is free, on the soft determinist's definition of "free." It follows further that I am responsible for that behavior; or at least, that if I am not, it is not from any lack of freedom on my part.

But if the fulfillment of these conditions renders my behavior free — that is to say, if my behavior satisfies the conditions of free action set forth in the theory of soft determinism — then my behavior will be no less free if we assume further conditions that are perfectly consistent with those already satisfied.

We suppose further, accordingly, that while my behavior is entirely in accordance with my own volitions, and thus "free" in terms of the conception of freedom we are examining, my volitions themselves are caused. To make this graphic, we can suppose that an ingenious physiologist can induce in me any volition he pleases, simply by pushing various buttons on an instrument to which, let us suppose, I am attached by numerous wires. All the volitions I have in that situation are, accordingly, precisely the ones he gives me. By pushing one button, he evokes in me the volition to raise my hand; and my hand, being unimpeded, rises in response to that volition. By pushing another, he induces the volition in me to kick, and my foot, being unimpeded, kicks in response to that volition. We can even suppose that the physiologist puts a rifle in my hands, aims it at some passerby, and then, by pushing the proper button, evokes in me the volition to squeeze my finger against the trigger, whereupon the passerby falls dead of a bullet wound.

This is the description of a man who is acting in accordance with his inner volitions, a man whose body is unimpeded and unconstrained in its motions, these motions being the effects of those inner states. It is hardly the description of a free and responsible agent. It is the perfect description of a puppet. To render someone your puppet, it is not necessary forcibly to constrain the motions of his limbs, after the fashion that real puppets are moved. A subtler but no less effective means of making a person your puppet would be to gain complete control of his inner states, and ensuring, as the theory of soft determinism does ensure, that his body will move in accordance with them.

The example is somewhat unusual, but it is no worse for that. It is perfectly intelligible, and it does appear to refute the soft determinist's conception of freedom. One might think that, in such a case, the agent should not have allowed himself to be so rigged in the first place, but this is irrelevant; we can suppose that he was not aware that he was and was hence unaware of the source of those inner states that prompted his bodily motions. The example can, moreover, be modified in perfectly realistic ways, so as to coincide with actual and familiar cases. One can, for instance, be given a compulsive desire for certain drugs, simply by having them administered over a course of time. Suppose, then, that I do, with neither my knowledge nor consent, thus become a victim of such a desire and act upon it. Do I act freely, merely by virtue of the fact that I am unimpeded in my quest for drugs? In a sense I do, surely, but I am hardly free with respect to whether or not I shall use drugs. I never chose to have the desire for them inflicted upon me.

Nor does it, of course, matter whether the inner states that allegedly prompt all my "free" activity are evoked in me by another agent or by perfectly impersonal forces. Whether a desire that causes my body to behave in a certain way is inflicted upon me by another person, for instance, or derived from hereditary factors, or indeed from anything at all, matters not the least. In any case, if it is in fact the cause of my bodily behavior, I cannot help but act in accordance with it. Wherever it came from, whether from personal or impersonal origins, it was entirely caused or determined, and not within my control. Indeed, if determinism is true, as the theory of soft determinism holds it to be, all those inner states that cause my body to behave in whatever ways it behaves must arise from circumstances that existed before I was born; for the chain of causes and effects is infinite, and none could have been the least different, given those that preceded.

SIMPLE INDETERMINISM

We might at first now seem warranted in simply denying determinism, and saying that, insofar as they are free, my actions are not caused; or that, if they are caused by my own inner states — my own desires, impulses, choices, volitions, and whatnot — then these, in any case, are not caused. This is a perfectly clear sense in which a person's action, assuming that it was free, could have been otherwise. If it was uncaused, then, even given the conditions under which it occurred and all that preceded, some other act was nonetheless possible, and he did not have to do what he did. Or if his action was the inevitable consequence of his own inner states, and could not have been otherwise, given these, we can nevertheless say that these inner states, being uncaused, could have been otherwise, and could thereby have produced different actions.

Only the slightest consideration will show, however, that this simple denial of determinism has not the slightest plausibility. For let us suppose it is true, and that some of my bodily motions — namely, those that I regard as my free acts — are not caused at all or, if caused by my own inner states, that these are not caused. We shall thereby avoid picturing a puppet, to be sure — but only by substituting something even less like a human being; for the conception that now emerges is not that of a free person, but of an erratic and jerking phantom, without any rhyme or reason at all.

Suppose that my right arm is free, according to this conception; that is, that its motions are uncaused. It moves this way and that from time to time, but nothing causes these motions. Sometimes it moves forth vigorously, sometimes up, sometimes down, sometimes it just drifts vaguely about — these motions all being wholly free and uncaused. Manifestly I have nothing to do with them at all; they just happen, and neither I nor anyone can ever tell what this arm will be doing next. It might seize a club and lay it on the head of the nearest bystander, no less to my astonishment than his. There will never be any point in asking why these motions occur, or in seeking any explanation of them, for under the conditions assumed there is no explanation. They just happen, from no causes at all.

This is no description of free, voluntary, or responsible behavior. Indeed, so far as the motions of my body or its parts are entirely uncaused, such motions cannot even be ascribed to me as my behavior in the first place, since I have nothing to do with them. The behavior of my arm is just the random motion of a foreign object. Behavior that is mine must be behavior that is within my control, but motions that occur from no causes are beyond the control of anyone. I can have no more to do with, and no more control over, the uncaused motions of my limbs than a gambler has over the motions of an honest roulette wheel. I can only, like him, idly wait to see what happens.

Nor does it improve things to suppose that my bodily motions are caused by my own inner states, so long as we suppose these to be wholly uncaused. The result will be the same as before. My arm, for example, will move this way and that, sometimes up and sometimes down, sometimes vigorously and sometimes just drifting about, always in response to certain inner states, to be sure. But since these are supposed to be wholly uncaused, it follows that I have no control over them and hence none over their effects. If my hand lays a club forcefully on the nearest bystander, we can indeed say that this motion resulted from an inner club-wielding desire of mine; but we must add that I had nothing to do with that desire, and that it arose, to be followed by its inevitable effect, no less to my astonishment than to his. Things like this do, alas, sometimes happen. We are all sometimes seized by compulsive impulses that arise we know not whence, and we do sometimes act upon these. But because they are far from being examples of free, voluntary, and responsible behavior, we need only to learn that the behavior was of this sort to conclude that it was not free, voluntary, or responsible. It was erratic, impulsive, and irresponsible.

DETERMINISM AND SIMPLE INDETERMINISM AS THEORIES

Both determinism and simple indeterminism are loaded with difficulties, and no one who has thought much on them can affirm either of them without some embarrassment. Simple indeterminism has nothing whatever to be said for it, except that it appears to remove the grossest difficulties of determinism, only, however, to imply perfect absurdities of its own. Determinism, on the other hand, is at least initially plausible. People seem to have a natural inclination to believe in it; it is, indeed, almost required for the very exercise of practical intelligence. And beyond this, our experience appears always to confirm it, so long as we are dealing with everyday facts of common experience, as distinguished from the esoteric researches of theoretical physics. But determinism, as applied to human behavior, has implications that few can casually accept, and they appear to be implications that no modification of the theory can efface.

Both theories, moreover, appear logically irreconcilable to the two items of data that we set forth at the outset; namely, (1) that my behavior is sometimes the outcome of my deliberation, and (2) that in these and other cases it is sometimes up to me what I do. Because these were our data, it is important to see, as must already be quite clear, that these theories cannot be reconciled to them.

I can deliberate only about my own future actions, and then only if I do not already know what I am going to do. If a certain nasal tickle warns me that I am about to sneeze, for instance, then I cannot deliberate whether to sneeze or not; I can only prepare for the impending convulsion. But if determinism is true, then there are always conditions existing antecedently to everything I do, sufficient for my doing just that, and such as to render it inevitable. If I can know what those conditions are and what behavior they are sufficient to produce, then I can in every such case know what I am going to do and cannot then deliberate about it.

By itself this only shows, of course, that I can deliberate only in ignorance of the causal conditions of my behavior; it does not show that such conditions cannot exist. It is odd, however, to suppose that deliberation should be a mere substitute for clear knowledge. Ignorance is a condition of speculation, inference, and guesswork, which have nothing whatever to do with deliberation. A prisoner awaiting execution may not know when he is going to die, and he may even entertain the hope of reprieve, but he cannot deliberate about this. He can only speculate, guess — and wait.

Worse yet, however, it now becomes clear that I cannot deliberate about what I am going to do, if it is even *possible* for me to find out in advance, whether I do in fact find out in advance or not. I can deliberate only with the view to deciding what to do, to making up my mind; and this is impossible if I believe that it could be inferred what I am going to do from conditions already existing, even though I have not made that inference myself. If I believe that what I am going to do has been rendered inevitable by conditions already existing, and could be inferred by anyone having the requisite sagacity, then I cannot try to decide whether to do it or not, for there is simply nothing left to decide. I can at best only guess or try to figure it out myself or, all prognostics failing, I can wait and see; but I cannot deliberate. I deliberate in order to *decide* what *to* do, not to *discover* what it is that I am *going* to do. But if determinism is true, then there are always antecedent conditions sufficient for everything that I do, and this can always be inferred by anyone having the requisite sagacity; that is, by anyone having a knowledge of what those conditions are and what behavior they are sufficient to produce.

This suggests what in fact seems quite clear, that determinism cannot be reconciled with our second datum either, to the effect that it is sometimes up to me what I am going to do. For if it is ever really up to me whether to do this thing or that, then, as we have seen, each alternative course of action must be such that I can do it; not that I can do it in some abstruse or hypothetical sense of "can"; not that I could do it if only something were true that is not true; but in the sense that it is then and there within my power to do it. But this is never so, if determinism is true, for on the very formulation of that theory whatever happens at any time is the only thing that can then happen, given all that precedes it. It is simply a logical consequence of this that whatever I do at any time is the only thing I can then do, given the conditions that precede my doing it. Nor does it help in the least to interpose, among the causal antecedents of my behavior, my own inner states, such as my desires, choices, acts of will, and so on. For even supposing these to be always involved in voluntary behavior — which is highly doubtful in itself — it is a consequence of determinism that these, whatever they are at any time, can never be other than what they then are. Every chain of causes and effects, if determinism is true, is infinite. This is why it is not now up to me whether I shall a moment hence be male or female. The conditions determining my sex have existed through my whole life, and even prior to my life. But if determinism is true, the same holds of anything that I ever am, ever become, or ever do. It matters not whether we are speaking of the most patent facts of my being, such as my sex; or the most subtle, such as my feelings, thoughts, desires, or choices. Nothing could be other than it is, given what was; and while we may indeed say, quite idly, that something — some inner state of mind, for instance — *could* have been different, had only something *else* been different, any consolation of this thought evaporates as soon as we add that whatever would have to have been different could not have been different.

It is even more obvious that our data cannot be reconciled to the theory of simple indeterminism. I can deliberate only about my own actions; this is obvious. But the random, uncaused motion of any body whatever, whether it be a part of my body or not, is no action of mine and nothing that is within my power. I might try to guess what these motions will be, just as I might try to guess how a roulette wheel will behave, but I cannot deliberate about them or try to decide what they shall be, simply because these things are not up to me. Whatever is not caused by anything is not caused by me, and nothing could be more plainly inconsistent with saying that it is nevertheless up to me what it shall be.

THE THEORY OF AGENCY

The only conception of action that accords with our data is one according to which people — and perhaps some other things too — are sometimes, but of course not always, self-determining beings; that is, beings that are sometimes the causes of their own behavior. In the case of an action that is free, it must not only be such that it is caused by the agent who performs it, but also such that no antecedent conditions were sufficient for his performing just that action. In the case of an action that is both free and rational, it must be such that the agent who performed it did so for some reason, but this reason cannot have been the cause of it.

Now, this conception fits what people take themselves to be; namely, beings who act, or who are agents, rather than beings that are merely acted upon, and whose behavior is simply the causal consequence of conditions that they have not wrought. When I believe that I have done something, I do believe that it was I who caused it to be done, I who made something happen, and not merely something within me, such as one of my own subjective states, which is not identical with myself. If I believe that something not identical with myself was the cause of my behavior — some event wholly external to myself, for instance, or even one internal to myself, such as a nerve impulse, volition, or whatnot — then I cannot regard that behavior as being an act of mine, unless I further believe that I was the cause of that external or internal event. My pulse, for example, is caused and regulated by certain conditions existing within me, and not by myself. I do not, accordingly, regard this activity of my body as my action, and would be no more tempted to do so if I became suddenly conscious within myself of those conditions or impulses that produce it. This is behavior with which I have nothing to do, behavior that is not within my immediate control, behavior that is not only not free activity, but not even the activity of an agent to begin with; it is nothing but a mechanical reflex. Had I never learned that my very life depends on this pulse beat, I would regard it with complete indifference, as something foreign to me, like the oscillations of a clock pendulum that I idly contemplate.

Now this conception of activity, and of an agent who is the cause of it, involves two rather strange metaphysical notions that are never applied elsewhere in nature. The first is that of a *self* or *person* — for example, a man — who is not merely a collection of things or events, but a self-moving being. For on this view it is a person, and not merely some part of him or something within him, that is the cause of his own activity. Now, we certainly do not know that a human being is anything more than an assemblage of physical things and processes that act in accordance with those laws that describe the behavior of all other physical things and processes. Even though he is a living being, of enormous complexity, there is nothing, apart from the requirements of this theory, to suggest that his behavior is so radically different in its origin from that of other physical objects, or that an understanding of it must be sought in some metaphysical realm wholly different from that appropriate to the understanding of nonliving things.

Second, this conception of activity involves an extraordinary conception of causation according to which an agent, which is a substance and not an event, can nevertheless be the cause of an event. Indeed, if he is a free agent then he can, on this conception, cause an event to occur — namely, some act of his own — without anything else causing him to do so. This means that an agent is sometimes a cause, without being an antecedent sufficient condition; for if I affirm that I am the cause of some act of mine, then I am plainly not saying that my very existence is sufficient for its occurrence, which would be absurd. If I say that my hand causes my pencil to move, then I am saying that the motion of my hand is, under the other conditions then prevailing, sufficient for the motion of the pencil. But if I then say that I cause my hand to move, I am not saying anything remotely like this, and surely not that the motion of my self is sufficient for the motion of my arm and hand, since these are the only things about me that are moving.

This conception of the causation of events by things that are not events is, in fact, so different from the usual philosophical conception of a cause that it should not even bear the same name, for "being a cause" ordinarily just means "being an antecedent sufficient condition or set of conditions." Instead, then, of speaking of agents as *causing* their own acts, it would perhaps be better to use another word entirely, and say, for instance, that they *originate* them, *initiate* them, or simply that they *perform* them.

Now this is, on the face of it, a dubious conception of what a person is. Yet it is consistent with our data, reflecting the presuppositions of deliberation, and appears to be the only conception that is consistent with them, as determinism and simple indeterminism are not. The theory of agency avoids the absurdities of simple indeterminism by conceding that human behavior is caused, while at the same time avoiding the difficulties of determinism by denying that every chain of causes and effects is infinite. Some such causal chains, on this view, have beginnings, and they begin with agents themselves. Moreover, if we are to suppose that it is sometimes up to me what I do, and understand this in a sense that is not consistent with determinism, we must suppose that I am an agent or a being who initiates his own actions, sometimes under conditions that do not determine what action I shall perform. Deliberation becomes, on this view, something that is not only possible but quite rational, for it does make sense to deliberate about activity that is truly my own and that depends in its outcome upon me as its author, and not merely upon something more or less esoteric that is supposed to be intimately associated with me, such as my thoughts, volitions, choices or whatnot.

One can hardly affirm such a theory of agency with complete comfort, however, and not wholly without embarrassment, for the conception of agents and their powers which is involved in it is strange indeed, if not positively mysterious. In fact, one can hardly be blamed here for simply denying our data outright, rather than embracing this theory to which they do most certainly point. Our data — to the effect that we do sometimes deliberate before acting, and that, when we do, we presuppose among other things that it is up to us what we are going to do — rest upon nothing more than fairly common consent. These data might simply be illusions. It might, in fact, be that no one ever deliberates but only imagines that he does, that from pure conceit he supposes himself to be the master of his behavior and the author of his acts. Spinoza has suggested that if a stone, having been thrown into the air, were suddenly to become conscious, it would suppose itself to be the source of its own motion, being then conscious of what it was doing but not aware of the real cause of its behavior. Certainly we are *sometimes* mistaken in believing that we are behaving as a result of choice deliberately arrived at. A man might, for example, easily imagine that his embarking upon matrimony is the result of the most careful and rational deliberation, when in fact the causes, perfectly sufficient for that behavior, might be of an entirely physiological, unconscious origin. If it is sometimes false that we deliberate and then act as the result of a decision deliberately arrived at, even when we suppose it to be true, it might always be false. No one seems able, as we have noted, to describe deliberation without metaphors, and the conception of a thing's being "within one's power" or "up to him" seems to defy analysis or definition altogether, if taken in a sense that the theory of agency appears to require.

These are, then, dubitable conceptions, despite their being so well implanted in common sense. Indeed, when we turn to the theory of fatalism, we shall find formidable metaphysical considerations that appear to rule them out altogether. Perhaps here, as elsewhere in metaphysics, we should be content with discovering difficulties, with seeing what is and what is not consistent with such convictions as we happen to have, and then drawing such satisfaction as we can from the realization that, no matter where we begin, the world is mysterious and that we who try to understand it are even more so. This realization can, with some justification, make one feel wise, even in the full realization of his ignorance.

CHAPTER SIX

Fate

We are all, at certain moments of pain, threat, or bereavement, apt to entertain the idea of fatalism, the thought that what is happening at a particular moment is unavoidable, that we are powerless to prevent it. Sometimes we find ourselves in circumstances not of our own making, in which our very being and destinies are so thoroughly anchored that the thought of fatalism can be quite overwhelming, and sometimes consoling. One feels that whatever then happens, however good or ill, will be what those circumstances yield, and we are helpless. Soldiers, it is said, are sometimes possessed by such thoughts. Perhaps everyone would feel more inclined to them if they paused once in a while to think of how little they ever had to do with bringing themselves to wherever they have arrived in life, how much of their fortunes and destinies were decided for them by sheer circumstance, and how the entire course of their lives is often set, once and for all, by the most trivial incidents, which they did not produce and could not even have foreseen. If we are free to work out our destinies at all, which is doubtful, we have a freedom that is at best exercised within exceedingly narrow paths. All the important things — when we are born, or what parents, into what culture, whether we are loved or rejected, whether we are male or female, our temperament, our intelligence or stupidity, indeed, everything that makes for the bulk of our happiness and misery — all these are decided for us by the most casual and indifferent circumstances, by sheer coincidences, chance encounters, and seemingly insignificant fortuities. One can see this in retrospect if he searches, but few search. The fate that has given us our very being has given us also our pride and conceit, and has thereby formed us so that, being human, we congratulate ourselves on our blessings, which we call our achievements; blame the world for our blunders, which we call our misfortunes; and scarcely give a thought to that impersonal fate that arbitrarily dispenses both.

FATALISM AND DETERMINISM

Determinism, it will be recalled, is the theory that all events are rendered unavoidable by their causes. The attempt is sometimes made to distinguish this from fatalism by saying that, according to the fatalist, certain events are going to happen *no matter what*, or in other words, regardless of causes. But this is enormously contrived. It would be hard to find in the whole history of thought a single fatalist, on that conception of it.

Fatalism is the belief that whatever happens is unavoidable. That is the clearest expression of the doctrine, and it provides the basis of the attitude of calm acceptance that the fatalist is thought, quite correctly, to embody. One who endorses the claim of universal causation, then, and the theory of the causal determination of all human behavior, is a kind of fatalist — or at least he should be, if he is consistent. For that theory, as we have seen, once it is clearly spelled out and not hedged about with unresolved "ifs," does entail that whatever happens is rendered inevitable by the causal conditions preceding it, and is therefore unavoidable. One can indeed think of verbal formulas for distinguishing the two theories, but if we think of a fatalist as one who has a certain attitude, we find it to be the attitude that a thoroughgoing determinist should, in consistency, assume. That some philosophical determinists are not fatalists does not so much illustrate a great difference between fatalism and determinism but rather the humiliation to one's pride that a fatalist position can deliver, and the comfort that can sometimes be found in evasion.

FATALISM WITH RESPECT TO THE FUTURE
AND THE PAST

A fatalist, then, is someone who believes that whatever happens is and always was unavoidable. He thinks it is not up to him what will happen a thousand years hence, next year, tomorrow, or the very next moment. Of course he does not pretend always to *know* what is going to happen. Hence, he might try sometimes to read signs and portents, as meteorologists and astrologers do, or to contemplate the effects upon him of the various things that might, for all he knows, be fated to occur. But he does not suppose that whatever happens could ever have really been avoidable.

A fatalist thus thinks of the future in the way we all think of the past, for everyone is a fatalist as he looks *back* on things. To a large extent we know what has happened — some of it we can even remember — whereas the future is still obscure to us, and we are therefore tempted to imbue it, in our imagination, with all sorts of "possibilities." The fatalist resists this temptation, knowing that mere ignorance can hardly give rise to any genuine possibility in things. He thinks of both past and future "under the aspect of eternity," the way God is supposed to view them. We all think of the past this way, as something settled and fixed, to be taken for what it is. We are never in the least tempted to try to modify it. It is not in the least up to us what happened last year, yesterday, or even a moment ago, any more than are the motions of the heavens or the political developments in Tibet. If we are not fatalists, then we might think that past things once *were* up to us, to bring about or prevent, as long as they were still future — but this expresses our attitude toward the future, not the past.

Such is surely our conception of the whole past, whether near or remote. But the consistent fatalist thinks of the future in the same way. We say of past things that they are no longer within our power. The fatalist says they never were.

THE SOURCES OF FATALISM

A fatalistic way of thinking most often arises from theological ideas, or from what are generally thought to be certain presuppositions of science and logic. Thus, if God is really all-knowing and all-powerful, it is not hard to suppose that He has arranged for everything to happen just as it is going to happen, that He already knows every detail of the whole future course of the world, and there is nothing left for you and me to do except watch things unfold, in the here or the hereafter. But without bringing God into the picture, it is not hard to suppose, as we have seen, that everything that happens is wholly determined by what went before it, and hence that whatever happens at any future time is the only thing that can then happen, given what precedes it. Or even disregarding that, it seems natural to suppose that there is a body of truth concerning what the future holds, just as there is such truth concerning what is contained in the past, whether or not it is known to any person or even to God, and hence, that everything asserted in that body of truth will assuredly happen, in the fullness of time, precisely as it is described therein.

No one needs to be convinced that fatalism is the only proper way to view the past. That it is also the proper way to view the future is less obvious, due in part, perhaps, to our vastly greater ignorance of what the future holds. The consequences of holding such fatalistic views are obviously momentous. To say nothing of the consolation of fatalism, which enables a person to view all things as they arise with the same undisturbed mind with which he contemplates even the most revolting of history's horrors, the fatalist teaching also relieves one of all tendency toward both blame and approbation of others and of both guilt and conceit in himself. It promises that a perfect understanding is possible and removes the temptation to view things in terms of human wickedness and moral responsibility. This thought alone, once firmly grasped, yields a sublime acceptance of all that life and nature offer, whether to oneself or one's fellows; and although it thereby reduces one's pride, it simultaneously enhances the feelings, opens the heart, and expands the understanding.

DIVINE OMNISCIENCE

Suppose for the moment, just for the purpose of this discussion, that God exists and is omniscient. To say that God is omniscient means that He knows everything that is true. He cannot, of course, know that which is false. Concerning any falsehood, an omniscient being can know that it is false; but then it is a truth that is known, namely, the truth that the thing in question *is* a falsehood. So if it is false that the moon is a cube, then God can, like you or me, know that this is false; but He cannot know the falsehood itself, that the moon is a cube.

Thus, if God is omniscient He knows, as you probably do, the date of your birth. He also knows, as you may not, the hour of your birth. Furthermore, God knows, as you assuredly do not, the date of your conception — for there is such a truth, and we are supposing that God knows every truth. Moreover, He knows, as you surely do not, the date of your death, and the circumstances thereof — whether at that moment, known already to Him, you die as the result of an accident, a fatal malady, suicide, murder, whatever. And, still assuming God exists and knows everything, He knows whether any ant walked across my desk last night, and if so, what ant it was, where it came from, how long it was on the desk, how it came to be there, and so on, to every truth about this insect that there is. Similarly, of course, He knows when some ant will again appear on my desk, if ever. He knows the number of hairs on my head, notes the fall of every sparrow, knows why it fell, and why it was going to fall. These are simply a few of the consequences of the omniscience that we are for the moment assuming. A more precise way of expressing all this is to say that God knows, concerning any statement whatever that anyone could formulate, that it is true, in case it is, and otherwise, that it is false. And let us suppose that God, at some time or other, or perhaps from time to time, vouchsafes some of his knowledge to people, or perhaps to certain chosen persons. Thus prophets arise, proclaiming the coming of certain events, and things do then happen as they have foretold. Of course it is not surprising that they should, on the supposition we are making; namely, that the foreknowledge of these things comes from God, who is omniscient.

THE STORY OF OSMO

Now, then, let us make one further supposition, which will get us squarely into the philosophical issue these ideas are intended to introduce. Let us suppose that God has revealed a particular set of facts to a chosen scribe who, believing (correctly) that they came from God, wrote them all down. The facts in question then turned out to be all the more or less significant episodes in the life of some perfectly ordinary man named Osmo. Osmo was entirely unknown to the scribe, and in fact to just about everyone, but there was no doubt concerning whom all these facts were about, for the very first thing received by the scribe from God, was: "He of whom I speak is called Osmo." When the revelations reached a fairly voluminous bulk and appeared to be completed, the scribe arranged them in chronological order and assembled them into a book. He at first gave it the title *The Life of Osmo, as Given by God*, but thinking that people would take this to be some sort of joke, he dropped the reference to God.

The book was published but attracted no attention whatsoever, because it appeared to be nothing more than a record of the dull life of a very plain man named Osmo. The scribe wondered, in fact, why God had chosen to convey such a mass of seemingly pointless trivia.

The book eventually found its way into various libraries, where it gathered dust until one day a high school teacher in Indiana, who rejoiced under the name of Osmo, saw a copy on the shelf. The title caught his eye. Curiously picking it up and blowing the dust off, he was thunderstruck by the opening sentence: "Osmo is born in Mercy Hospital in Auburn, Indiana, on June 6, 1965, of Finnish parentage, and after nearly losing his life from an attack of pneumonia at the age of five, he is enrolled in the St. James school there." Osmo turned pale. The book nearly fell from his hands. He thumbed back in excitement to discover who had written it. Nothing was given of its authorship nor, for that matter, of its publisher. His questions of the librarian produced no further information, he being as ignorant as Osmo of how the book came to be there.

So Osmo, with the book pressed tightly under his arm, dashed across the street for some coffee, thinking to compose himself and then examine this book with care. Meanwhile he glanced at a few more of its opening remarks, at the things said there about his difficulties with his younger sister, how he was slow in learning to read, of the summer on Mackinac Island, and so on. His emotions now somewhat quieted, Osmo began a close reading. He noticed that everything was expressed in the present tense, the way newspaper headlines are written. For example, the text read, "Osmo is born in Mercy Hospital," instead of saying he *was* born there, and it recorded that he quarrels with his sister, is a slow student, is fitted with dental braces at age eight, and so on, all in the journalistic present tense. But the text itself made quite clear approximately when all these various things happened, for everything was in chronological order, and in any case each year of its subject's life constituted a separate chapter and was so titled — "Osmo's Seventh Year," "Osmo's Eighth Year," and so on through the book.

Osmo became absolutely engrossed, to the extent that he forgot his original astonishment, bordering on panic, and for a while even lost his curiosity concerning authorship. He sat drinking coffee and reliving his childhood, much of which he had all but forgotten until the memories were revived by the book now before him. He had almost forgotten about the kitten, for example, and had entirely forgotten its name, until he read, in the chapter called "Osmo's Seventh Year," this observation: "Sobbing, Osmo takes Fluffy, now quite dead, to the garden, and buries her next to the rose bush." Ah yes! And then there was Louise, who sat next to him in the eighth grade — it was all right there. And how he got caught smoking one day. And how he felt when his father died. On and on. Osmo became so absorbed that he quite forgot the business of the day, until it occurred to him to turn to Chapter 26, to see what might be said there, he having just recently turned twenty-six. He had no sooner done so than his panic returned, for lo! what the book said was *true!* That it rains on his birthday for example, that his wife fails to give him the binoculars he had hinted he would like, that he receives a raise in salary shortly thereafter, and so on. Now how in God's name, Osmo pondered, could anyone know that apparently before it had happened? For these were quite recent events, and the book had dust on it. Quickly moving on, Osmo came to this: "Sitting and reading in the coffee shop across from the library, Osmo, perspiring copiously, entirely forgets, until it is too late, that he was supposed to collect his wife at the hairdresser's at four." Oh my god! He had forgotten all about that. Yanking out his watch, Osmo discovered that it was nearly five o'clock — too late. She would be on her way home by now, and in a very sour mood.

Osmo's anguish at this discovery was nothing, though, compared with what the rest of the day held for him. He poured more coffee, and it now occurred to him to check the number of chapters in this amazing book: only twenty-nine! But surely, he thought, that doesn't mean anything. How anyone could have gotten all this stuff down so far was puzzling enough, to be sure, but no one on God's earth could possibly know in advance how long this or that person is going to live. (Only God could know that sort of thing, Osmo reflected.) So he read along; though not without considerable uneasiness and even depression, for the remaining three chapters were on the whole discouraging. He thought he had gotten that ulcer under control, for example. And he didn't see any reason to suppose his job was going to turn out that badly, or that he was really going to break a leg skiing; after all, he could just give up skiing. But then the book ended on a terribly dismal note. It said: "And Osmo, having taken Northwest flight 569 from O'Hare, perishes when the aircraft crashes on the runway at Fort Wayne, with considerable loss of life, a tragedy rendered the more calamitous by the fact that Osmo had neglected to renew his life insurance before the expiration of the grace period." And that was all. That was the end of the book.

So *that's* why it had only twenty-nine chapters. Some idiot thought he was going to get killed in a plane crash. But, Osmo thought, he just wouldn't get on that plane. And this would also remind him to keep his insurance in force.

(About three years later our hero, having boarded a flight for St. Paul, went berserk when the pilot announced they were going to land at Fort Wayne instead. According to one of the flight attendants, he tried to hijack the aircraft and divert it to another airfield. The Civil Aeronautics Board cited the resulting disruptions as contributing to the crash that followed as the plane tried to land.)

FOUR QUESTIONS

Osmo's extraordinary circumstances led him to embrace the doctrine of fatalism. Not quite completely, perhaps, for there he was, right up to the end, trying vainly to buck his fate — trying, in effect, to make a fool of God, though he did not know this, because he had no idea of the book's source. Still, he had the overwhelming evidence of his whole past life to make him think that everything was going to work out exactly as described in the book. It always had. It was, in fact, precisely this conviction that terrified him so.

But now let us ask these questions, in order to make Osmo's experiences more relevant to our own. First, why did he become, or nearly become, a fatalist? Second, just what did his fatalism amount to? Third, was his belief justified in terms of the evidence he had? And finally, is that belief justified in terms of the evidence *we* have — or in other words, should we be fatalists too?

This last, of course, is the important metaphysical question, but we have to approach it through the others.

Why did Osmo become a fatalist? Osmo became a fatalist because there existed a set of true statements about the details of his life, both past and future, and he came to know what some of these statements were and to believe them, including many concerning his future. That is the whole of it.

No theological ideas entered into his conviction, nor any presuppositions about causal determinism, the coercion of his actions by causes, or anything of this sort. The foundations of Osmo's fatalism were entirely in logic and epistemology, having to do only with truth and knowledge. Ideas about God did not enter in, for he never suspected that God was the ultimate source of those statements. And at no point did he think God was *making* him do what he did. All he was concerned about was that someone seemed somehow to *know* what he had done and was going to do.

What, then, did Osmo believe? He did not, it should be noted, believe that certain things were going to happen to him *no matter what*. That does not express a logically coherent belief. He did not think he was in danger of perishing in an airplane crash even in case he did not get into any airplane, for example, or that he was going to break his leg skiing, whether he went skiing or not. No one believes what he considers to be plainly impossible. If anyone believes that a given event is going to happen, he does not doubt that those things necessary for its occurrence are going to happen too. The expression "no matter what," by means of which some philosophers have sought an easy and even childish refutation of fatalism, is accordingly highly inappropriate in any description of the fatalist conviction.

Osmo's fatalism was simply the realization that the things described in the book were unavoidable.

Of course we are all fatalists in this sense about some things, and the metaphysical question is whether this familiar attitude should not be extended to everything. We know the sun will rise tomorrow, for example, and there is nothing we can do about it. Each of us knows he is sooner or later going to die, too, and there is nothing to be done about that either. We normally do not know just when, of course, but it is mercifully so! For otherwise we would sit simply checking off the days as they passed, with growing despair, like a man condemned to the gallows and knowing the hour set for his execution. The tides ebb and flow, and heavens revolve, the seasons follow in order, generations arise and pass, and no one speaks of taking preventive measures. With respect to those things each of us recognizes as beyond his control, we are of necessity fatalists.

The question of fatalism is simply: Of all the things that happen in the world, which, if any, are avoidable? And the philosophical fatalist replies: None of them. They never were. Some of them only seemed so.

Was Osmo's fatalism justified? Of course it was. When he could sit right there and read a true description of those parts of his life that had not yet been lived, it would be idle to suggest to him that his future might, nonetheless, contain alternative possibilities. The only doubts Osmo had were whether those statements could really be true. But here he had the proof of his own experience, as one by one they were tested. Whenever he tried to prevent what was set forth, he of course failed. Such failure, over and over, of even the most herculean efforts, with never a single success, must surely suggest, sooner or later, that he was *destined* to fail. Even to the end, when Osmo tried so desperately to save himself from the destruction described in the book, his effort was totally in vain — as he should have realized it was going to be had he really known that what was said there was true. No power in heaven or earth can render false a statement that is true. It has never been done, and never will be.

Is the doctrine of fatalism, then, true? This amounts to asking whether our circumstances are significantly different from Osmo's. Of course we cannot read our own biographies the way he could. Only people who become famous ever have their lives recorded, and even so, it is always in retrospect. This is unfortunate. It is too bad that someone with sufficient knowledge — God, for example — cannot set down the lives of great men in advance, so that their achievements can be appreciated better by their contemporaries, and indeed, by their predecessors — their parents, for instance. But mortals do not have the requisite knowledge, and if there are any gods who do, they seem to keep it to themselves.

None of this matters, as far as our own fatalism is concerned. For the important thing to note is that, of the two considerations that explain Osmo's fatalism, only one of them was philosophically relevant, and that one applies to us no less than to him. The two considerations were: (1) there existed a set of true statements about his life, both past and future, and (2) he came to know what those statements were and to believe them. Now the second of these two considerations explains why, as a matter of psychological fact, Osmo became fatalistic, but it has nothing to do with the validity of that point of view. Its validity is assured by (1) alone. It was not the fact that the statements happened to be written down that rendered the things they described unavoidable; that had nothing to do with it at all. Nor was it the fact that, because they had been written, Osmo could read them. His reading them and coming to believe them likewise had nothing to do with the inevitability of what they described. This was ensured simply by there being such a set of statements, whether written or not, whether read by anyone or not, and whether or not known to be true. All that is required is that they should *be* true.

Each of us has but one possible past, described by that totality of statements about us in the past tense, each of which happens to be true. No one ever thinks of rearranging things there; it is simply accepted as given. But so also, each of us has but one possible future, described by that totality of statements about oneself in the future tense, each of which happens to be true. The sum of these constitutes one's biography. Part of it has been lived. The main outlines of it can still be seen, in retrospect, though most of its details are obscure. The other part has not been lived, though it most assuredly is going to be, in exact accordance with that set of statements just referred to. Some of its outlines can already be seen, in prospect, but it is on the whole more obscure than the part belonging to the past. We have at best only premonitory glimpses of it. It is no doubt for this reason that not all of this part, the part that awaits us, is perceived as given, and people do sometimes speak absurdly of altering it — as though what the future holds, as identified by any true statement in the future tense, might after all *not* hold.

Osmo's biography was all expressed in the present tense because all that mattered was that the things referred to were real events; it did not matter to what part of time they belonged. His past consisted of those things that preceded his reading of the book, and he simply accepted it as given. He was not tempted to revise what he said there, for he was sure it was true. But it took the book to make him realize that his future was also something given. It was equally pointless for him to try to revise what was said there, for it, too, was true. As the past contains what has happened, the future contains what will happen, and neither contains, in addition to these things, various other things that did not and will not happen.

Of course we know relatively little of what the future contains. Some things we know. We know the sun will go on rising and setting, for example, that taxes will be levied and wars will rage, that people will continue to be callous and greedy, and that people will be murdered and robbed. It is only the details that remain to be discovered. But the same is true of the past; it is only a matter of degree. When I meet a total stranger, I do not know, and will probably never know, what his past has been, beyond certain obvious things — that he had a mother, and things of this sort. I know nothing of the particulars of the vast realm of fact that is unique to his past. And the same for his future, with only this difference — that *all* people are strangers to me as far as their futures are concerned, and here I am even a stranger to myself.

Yet there is one thing I know concerning any stranger's past and the past of everything under the sun; namely, that whatever it might hold, there is nothing anyone can do about it now. What has happened cannot be undone. The mere fact that it has happened guarantees this.

And so it is, by the same token, of the future of everything under the sun. Whatever the future might hold, there is nothing anyone can do about it now. What will happen cannot be altered. The mere fact that it is going to happen guarantees this.

THE LAW OF EXCLUDED MIDDLE

The presupposition of fatalism is therefore nothing but the commonest presupposition of all logic and inquiry; namely, that there is such a thing as truth, and that this has nothing at all to do with the passage of time. Nothing *becomes* true or *ceases* to be true; whatever is truth at all simply *is* true.

It comes to the same thing, and is perhaps more precise, to say that every meaningful statement, whether about oneself or anything else, is either true or else it is false; that is, its denial is true. There is no middle ground. The principle is thus appropriately called *the law of excluded middle*. It has nothing to do with what tense a statement happens to express, nor with the question whether anyone, man or god, happens to know whether it is true or false.

Thus no one knows whether there was an ant on my desk last night, and no one ever will. But we do know that either this statement is true or else its denial is true — there is no third alternative. If we say it *might* be true, we mean only that we do not happen to know. Similarly, no one knows whether or not there is going to be an ant there tonight, but we do know that either it will or else it will not be there.

In a similar way we can distinguish two mutually exclusive but exhaustive classes of statements about any person; namely, the class of all those that are true, and the class of all that are false. There are no others in addition to these. Included in each are statements never asserted or even considered by anyone, but such that, if anyone were to formulate one of them, it would either be a true statement or else a false one.

Consider, then, that class of statements about some particular person — you, let us suppose — each of which happens to be true. Their totality constitutes your biography. One combination of such statements describes the time, place, and circumstances of your birth. Another combination describes the time, place, and circumstances of your death. Others describe in detail the rises and falls of your fortunes, your achievements and failures, your joys and sorrows — absolutely everything that is true of you.

Some of these things you have already experienced, others await you. But the entire biography is there. It is not written, and probably never will be; but it is nevertheless there, all of it. If, like Osmo, you had some way of discovering those statements in advance, then like him you could hardly help becoming a fatalist. But foreknowledge of the truth would not create any truth, nor invest your philosophy with truth, nor add anything to the philosophical foundations of the fatalism that would then be so apparent to you. It would only serve to make it apparent.

OBJECTIONS

This thought, and the sense of its force, have tormented and frightened people from the beginning, and thinkers whose pride sometimes exceeds their acumen and their reverence for truth have attempted every means imaginable to demolish it. There are few articles of faith upon which virtually everyone can agree, but one of them is certainly the belief in their cherished free will. Any argument in opposition to the doctrine of fate, however feeble, is immediately and uncritically embraced, as though the refutation of fatalism required only the denial of it, supported by reasons that would hardly do credit to a child. It will be worthwhile, therefore, to look briefly at some of the arguments most commonly heard.

1. One can neither foresee the future nor prove that there is any god, or even if there is, that he could know in advance the free actions of men.

   The reply to this is that it is irrelevant. The thesis of fatalism rests on no theory of divination and on no theology. These ideas were introduced only illustratively.

2. True statements are not the causes of anything. Statements only entail; they do not cause, and hence threaten no man's freedom.

   But this, too, is irrelevant, for the claim here denied is not one that has been made.

3. The whole argument just conflates fact and necessity into one and the same thing, treating as unavoidable that which is merely true. The fact that a given thing is

going to happen implies only that it is *going* to happen, not that is *has* to. Someone might still be able to prevent it — though of course no one will. For example, President Kennedy was murdered. This means it was true that he was going to be murdered. But it does not mean his death at that time and place was unavoidable. Someone *could* have rendered that statement false; though of course no one did.

That is probably the commonest "refutation" of fatalism ever offered. But how strong is the claim that something *can* be done, when in fact it never *has* been done in the whole history of the universe, in spite, sometimes, of the most strenuous efforts? No one has ever rendered false a statement that was true, however hard some have tried. When an attempt, perhaps a heroic attempt, is made to avoid a given calamity, and the thing in question happens anyway, at just the moment and in just the way it was going to happen, we have reason to doubt that it could have been avoided. And in fact great effort was made to save President Kennedy, for example, from the destruction toward which he was heading on that fatal day, a whole legion of bodyguards having no other mission. And it failed. True, we can say *if* more strenuous precautions had been taken, the event would not have happened. But to this we must add *true*, they were not taken, and hence *true*, they were not going to be taken — and we have on our hands again a true statement of the kind that no one has ever had the slightest degree of success in rendering false.

4. The fatalist argument just rests on a "confusion of modalities." The fact that something is true entails only that its denial is false, not that its denial is impossible. All that is impossible is that both should be true, or both false. Thus, if the president is going to be murdered, it is certainly false that he is not — but not impossible. What is impossible is that he will be both murdered and spared.

    Here again we have only a distracting irrelevancy, similar to the point just made. The fatalist argument has nothing to do with impossibility in those senses familiar to logic. It has to do with unavoidability. It is, in other words, concerned with human abilities. The fact that a statement is true does not, to be sure, entail that it is necessary, nor do all false statements express impossibilities. Nonetheless, no one is able to avoid what is truly described, however contingently, in any statement, nor to bring about what is thus falsely described. Nor can anyone convert the one to the other, making suddenly true that which was false, or vice versa. It has never been done, and it never will be. It would be a conceit indeed for someone now to suggest that he, alone among men, might be able to accomplish this feat. This inability goes far beyond the obvious impossibility of making something both true and false at once. No metaphysics turns on that simple point.

5. Perhaps it would be best, then, to discard the presupposition underlying the whole fatalist philosophy; namely, the idea that statements are true in advance of the things they describe. The future is the realm of possibilities, concerning any of which we should neither say it is true that it will happen, nor that it is false.

    But, in reply, this desperate move is nothing but arbitrary fiction, resorted to for no other reason than to be rid of the detested doctrine of fatalism. What is at issue here is the very law of excluded middle, which, it is suggested, we shall be allowed to affirm only up to that point at which it threatens something dear. We shall permit it to hold for one part of time, but suddenly retract it in speaking of another, even though the future is continuously being converted to the past through sheer temporal passage.

Most surely, if the statement, made now, that President Kennedy has been murdered, is a true one, then the prediction, made before the event, that he was going to be murdered, was true too. The two statements have exactly the same content, and are in fact one and the same statement, except for the variation of tense. The fact that this statement is more easily known in retrospect than in prospect casts no doubt on its truth but only illustrates a familiar fact of epistemology. A prediction, to be sure, must await fulfillment, but it does not thereupon for the first time acquire its truth. Indeed, had it not been true from the start, it could not have been fulfilled, nor its author congratulated for having it right. Fulfillment is nothing but the occurrence of what is correctly predicted.

The law of excluded middle is not like a blank check into which we can write whatever values we please, according to our preferences. We can no more make ourselves metaphysically free and masters of our destinies by adding qualifications to this law than a poor person can make himself rich just by adding figures to his bankbook. That law pronounces every meaningful statement true, or, if not true, then false. It leaves no handy peg between these two on which one may hang his beloved freedom of will for safekeeping, nor does it say anything whatever about time.

Every single philosophical argument against the teaching of fatalism rests upon the assumption that we are free to pursue and realize various alternative future possibilities — the very thing, of course, that is at issue. When some of these possibilities have become realized and moved on into the past, the supposed alternative possibilities usually appear to have been less real than they had seemed; but this somehow does not destroy the fond notion that they were there. Metaphysics and logic are weak indeed in the face of an opinion nourished by invincible pride, and most people would sooner lose their very souls than be divested of that dignity that they imagine rests upon their freedom of will.

INVINCIBLE FATE

We shall say, therefore, of whatever happens that it was going to be that way. And this is a comfort, both in fortune and in adversity. We shall say of him who turns out bad and mean that he was going to; of him who turns out happy and blessed that he was going to; neither praising nor berating fortune, crying over what has been, lamenting what was going to be, or passing moral judgments.

Shall we, then, sit idly by, passively observing the changing scene without participation, never testing our strength and our goodness, having no hand in what happens, or in making things come out as they should? This is a question for which each will find his own answer. Some people do little or nothing with their lives and might as well never have lived, they make such a waste of it. Others do much, and the lives of a few even shine like the stars. But we knew this before we ever began talking about fate. In time we will all know of which sort we were destined to be.

CHAPTER SEVEN

Space and Time

Few things have seemed more metaphysically puzzling than space and time. Each of these two terms seems to refer to something, yet it is impossible to find, in any ordinary way, what it is they refer to. If, as seems true, every real being must exist in space, or in time, or perhaps in both together, then what shall we say of space and time themselves? That they are not real beings? But how could we say that without implying the unreality of everything that exists within them?

Time, especially, has always been regarded by many philosophers as a dark subject of speculation, enigmatic and even incomprehensible. Part of this mysteriousness of time has resulted from thinking of it as something that *moves*, as when we speak, as all persons do, of the passage of time. Time seems to be presupposed whenever we speak of anything moving, since nothing can move or undergo any change whatever except over a brief or long period of time. So how, then, can time itself move?

It is partly out of rebellion against this notion of temporal passage, and all the difficulties this entails, that many metaphysicians have declared time to be unreal, to be some sort of illusion. Indeed, it is almost characteristic of metaphysicians to make this claim. Against the idea of a moving and hence paradoxical time they have set the idea of *eternity*, not as something that moves on and on endlessly, but rather as a kind of timelessness, wherein there is no changing, decaying, or dying, and wherein what is real is immutably so.

SIMILARITIES BETWEEN SPATIAL
AND TEMPORAL CONCEPTS

Before trying to fathom and unravel some of the more difficult problems of space and time and the differences between them, it will be useful to note their similarities. Some of these can be seen quite readily by noting that many of the same terms can be used and easily understood as expressing either spatial or temporal relationships.

The idea of being at a *place*, for example, can express either a spatial or a temporal idea, or both. If you speak of something as existing at Ivy, Virginia, for instance, you name its spatial place, and if you speak of it as existing on June 12, 1962, you name its place in time. By combining these you give, quite simply, its location in space and time. A corollary to this is the notion of a *distance* or an *interval*, which is easily used in either a spatial or a temporal sense. New York and Boston are spatially distant from each other, Plato and Kant are temporally so, because one can speak intelligibly of a long interval of time between these two. An allied notion is that of *being present*, which is, significantly, often used to express either the spatial concept of being *here* or the temporal concept of being *now*, or both. Again, the concept of *length* or *being extended* has a use in both contexts, though this is often overlooked. The expression "a length of time" has, in fact, a common use, and there is no more difficulty in understanding the idea of something lasting through a certain length of time than the idea of its extending through a certain length of space. The notion of length, in turn, leads to that of *parts*, which can be either spatial or temporal. Distinctions between the spatial parts of things are commonplace, but we sometimes also speak of the parts of a melody, or of a person's life. In fact, anything having temporal length, or duration in time, can be divided into temporal parts. The spatial parts of a thing are sometimes very similar to each other, as in the case of a brick wall, but so also are the temporal parts of something often quite similar to each other — for instance, those of a gravestone, which is much the same at one time as at another. Finally, it should be noted that the concept of a *physical object* involves both space and time, since any such object has, for instance, both kinds of length or extension and both kinds of parts. Some objects are spatially very small, like dust particles, and others are temporally so, like a flash of lightning; others are both, and some are neither.

THE COMPARISON OF SPATIAL
AND TEMPORAL RELATIONSHIPS

If one describes things in terms of such concepts as we have just illustrated he finds, often to his surprise, that the differences between their spatial and temporal relations are not as great as he might have supposed. It is intellectually stimulating and edifying to the understanding to see just how far such comparisons can sometimes be carried. A few examples will illustrate the point.

It will be noted that in formulating these comparisons we shall for the most part eschew the terms *space* and *time* and speak instead of *places* and *times*, and of *spatial* and *temporal relations*. This will help avoid the common error of thinking of space and time as strange, huge, and invisible substances but will still enable us to express whatever we wish to say on these subjects. Thus instead of describing two objects as "a mile apart in space," which suggests that there is a huge but invisible vessel called "space" in which these objects are contained, we can say instead that they are spatially separated by an interval of a mile, the word *interval* here quite properly suggesting not some sort of filament that holds the two things apart but rather a relationship between them. Similar modes of description can be used in speaking of time, such that we shall say how various things are temporally related to one another instead of speaking of certain events as "occurring in time." When we speak of particular *times* we shall be referring not to absolute moments in something called "time," but rather to the relations of certain parts of a clock to one another — for instance, the spatial relations of its "hands" to the numbers on its "face."

SOME COMPARATIVE EXAMPLES

It is often claimed that no object can be in two places at once, though it can occupy two or more times at one place, and some persons imagine that this expresses a very great and basic difference between the spatial and temporal relations of objects.

There are two ways in which an object can occupy two different times at only one place. It might simply remain where it is through an interval of time, or it might be removed from its place and later returned. Now it does at first seem as though nothing corresponding to these situations can ever happen the other way around; that is, that no object can be in two places at one time, and in particular that it cannot be returned to a time. When one tries to imagine situations that might be so described, he almost unavoidably finds himself thinking of two objects instead of one.

What must first be noted, however, is that an object can be in one place at two times only if it also occupies all the time in between, whether at that same place or another, and it must accordingly have some temporal length. Otherwise, we find that we are talking about two objects and not one. But with a similar provision, an object surely can be in two places at one time — by occupying the space between them as well. Someone who is standing with one foot in the doorway and the other outside is occupying two places at once, for instance. Of course it is tempting here to object that only a *part* of the person is in either place; he is not both entirely inside and entirely outside. But when this has been said, it must be remembered that it is a different *temporal* part of an object that, at a given place, occupies each of two or more times. Thus a person might just stay where he is for a while, and be in the same place at two different times — but it is not the same temporal part of the person that is at those two times. We have to remember that as things are more or less extended in space and have spatial boundaries, they are also extended in time and have temporal boundaries, defining their beginnings and endings. The intervals between such boundaries, of either kind, can be divided up into parts, both spatial and temporal. The comparison so far is, then, quite complete.

MOVING FORTH AND BACK
IN SPACE AND TIME

What about an object that moves from its place and then returns to it? This is easy enough to conceive, but can we think of anything similar to this with respect to a thing's temporal relations? Can something, for example, move from its time and return to it? Can anything, indeed, move in time at all?

The situation analogous to that of an object that moves from its place and later returns involves some particular details of description, but it is perfectly possible. An object can, accordingly, move forth and back "in time," just as it can "in space," provided one sees exactly what this means and sets forth descriptions in terms of the relationships involved.

To see this, we need only to give an exact description of an object that moves from its spatial location and then returns to it, which is easy enough, and then rewrite that description — substituting spatial terms for temporal terms, and vice versa. Our question, whether anything can move from its place in time and return to it, then becomes nothing but this question: Does our second description apply to anything that ever happens? It is important to see that this *is* what the question comes to, and not, at that point, lapse into imaginative but incoherent fables of science fiction.

Consider first, then, an object, O, which moves from its place and later returns to it. An exact description of this set of events is this:

1. O is at place$_1$ at time$_1$, and also at place$_1$ at time$_2$; it endures from time$_1$ through time$_2$, but is *then* (i.e., at some time within that temporal interval) at places other than place$_1$.

Now it can be seen that any object O whose behavior fits that description is one that moves from its place and returns to it, and one that, therefore, can be described as "moving forth and back in space."

Now let us rewrite that description, exchanging all spatial and temporal terms for each other, so as to have times where before we had places and vice versa. Doing this, we get the following description:

2. O is at time₁ at place₁ and also at time₁ at place₂; it extends from place₁ through place₂ but is *there* (*i.e.*, at some place within that spatial interval) at times other than time₁.

Before proceeding another step it must be noted that this is exactly the description we are looking for; that is, descriptions 1 and 2 should be carefully compared to see that they are the same, except that spatial and temporal concepts and relations have been switched around.

Does the second description, then, apply to anything that ever happens? That is, does anything ever behave in such a way as this? It is not hard to see that it does, and that an object can, accordingly, move forth and back in time just as well as it can in space. One will be inclined to reject this suggestion *only* if he departs from the description actually before him and begins reveling in incoherent fables, a temptation almost irresistible to most persons unaccustomed to thinking philosophically.

Consider, for example, something fairly well known, such as an earthquake. Suppose that at time₁ it occurs (simultaneously) in two nearby towns, which we may refer to as place₁ and place₂, and that it occurs everyplace between these two towns, but at one of those intermediate places at a time other than time₁. Such a set of events fits exactly our description 2. The earthquake, therefore, is something that (over an interval of space) moves forth and back in time; for this means nothing more than that it does fit that description.

Now some would want to insist here that more than one object is involved in this example, or even that an earthquake is no proper object at all. But it is an object in every significant way — it has a location in space and time, has interesting properties, such as the property of being destructive, and might even have a name, as hurricanes, for example, usually do. Nor is it to the point to suggest that, in the example given, more than one such object is involved. The people in the different towns could say, rightly, that they suffered from the same earthquake. Moreover, we can and ordinarily do say that moving about in space does not destroy the identity of a thing; no one would say, for instance, that if a chair is moved from one side of the room to the other and then back again it thereby becomes a different chair. And so, likewise, there is no reason for saying that moving about in time, in the manner suggested, destroys the identity of a thing. In the case of the chair, a temporal continuity is retained between its different temporal parts; it at no time, in the temporal interval in which it is moved, ceases to exist altogether. Similarly, the earthquake retains a spatial continuity between its different spatial parts; it at no place, in the spatial interval in which it moves, ceases to exist altogether. The analogies, then, seem quite complete.

TIME TRAVEL

A common device of imaginative story tellers is to have their characters move to a time long past or, even more imaginatively, to a time distantly future. Typically, someone steps into a time machine, much as one would step into a boat, and then, soon thereafter, finds himself surrounded by things and events that existed long ago or, in the case of a trip to the future, things that are still waiting to happen. Here the assumed similarity to a great "river of time" is obvious, for one can thus move up or down a river.

Such stories cannot, however, be understood as describing movement back or forth in time. The incoherence of such accounts is exposed in saying that, shortly thereafter — *i.e., at a later time* — someone finds himself living *at an earlier time*. To imagine "returning" to an earlier time is merely to imagine the recurrence of the events of that time. More precisely, it is to imagine everything *except oneself* just as it was then. One can, perhaps, imagine the world as it was long ago, imagine one's mother as a young woman in the surroundings then familiar to her, but it does not make sense to imagine oneself as a witness to all this, observing her as she matures, bears her children (oneself among them), and raises her family. Such words convey no coherent description.

TIME AND CHANGE

People have always thought of space and time as differing most markedly with respect to the way in which they are involved in the mutability of things. That is, time has always been thought of as an essential ingredient to motion and change, to the manner in which things arise and perish, flourish and decay, whereas there seems to be nothing quite comparable to this with respect to space. Change and time thus seem inseparable, whereas no such notion seems presupposed in the conception of space.

This way of looking at things is no more than a reflection of certain prejudices, however. Ordinarily when one thinks of motion and change he is thinking of temporal processes. Similarly, arising and perishing are thought of as events in time, and the descriptions of them are therefore appropriately tensed. Such ways of thinking and speaking do not, however, preclude the possibility of exactly analogous relationships in space, and when one attempts a description of such spatial change, he finds that it is not very difficult.

Ordinarily, to say that something *moves* means only that it occupies one place at one time and another place at another. But it obviously comes to exactly the same thing to say that it occupies one time at one place and another time at another. This kind of motion, then, which is referred to in Aristotelian philosophy as "local motion," is neither more nor less temporal than spatial; it is precisely both.

There is a more general sense of "change," however, according to which something is said to have a more or less interesting history. Something changes in this sense, in other words, in case it acquires and loses various properties and relationships over an interval of time — in case its temporal parts are dissimilar. But why may we not say, analogously, that a thing may acquire and lose various properties and relationships over an interval of space — or in other words, have spatial parts that are dissimilar? A thing would change *temporally*, in the sense we are considering, in case it was, for example, blue at one time and red at another. But then something, such as a wire, might be blue at one end and red at the other, and perhaps various other colors between these two places. This would accordingly be an example of *spatial* change. This sense of "change" is not, moreover, strange or unusual. It would make sense, for instance, to say of a wire, which was found to be red in one town and blue in another, that *somewhere* (not sometime) between those two places it changes color, and such change, like temporal change, might be gradual or abrupt, or in other words, occur over a long or brief interval.

THE FIXITY OF SPATIAL
OR TEMPORAL POSITIONS

Another way in which temporal and spatial relationships are widely thought to differ is expressed in the dictum that things can change their spatial positions but not their temporal ones, these being, once given, fixed eternally. Thus, something that is north of another can be moved around to the south of it, but something that is future to another cannot be "moved" around to its past. This is partly what is meant by speaking of time as irreversible, and it seems to have no parallel in space.

This way of looking at things, however, is again no more than a reflection of familiar habits of thought and speech, and it really amounts to very little once one sees beyond these. The claim, for example, that things cannot change their positions in time amounts to no more than the trivial claim that something cannot be in two times at once (at one time). It is thus comparable to the equally trivial claim that something cannot be in two places at one place. Similarly, the claim that two things, that are so related that the one is future to the other, are *always* so related is of course true, but again it is trivial. It is exactly comparable to a claim that two things that are related in such a way that one is north of the other are *everywhere* so related. The expressions "always" and "everywhere" in such statements add absolutely nothing to what is said in them. My son's birth belongs to a time future to my own birth, but it adds nothing to this to say that these events are "always" so related. Similarly, my son now happens to be several hundred miles east of me, but it adds nothing to this to say we are now "everywhere" so related.

SWITCHING SPATIAL
AND TEMPORAL POSITIONS

Here, however, we seem to run up against a great difference, for things seem able to switch their spatial positions but not their temporal ones. Thus, for example, something can be north of a given place, then move to the south of it. But can something be future to a given time, and move to the past of it? It seems not.

But here we need to look at the question more closely. And we note, first, that things can change their positions in space *only* over a lapse of time, because time is used up in moving from one place to another. This is so obvious that we tend to disregard it, but it is, in fact, crucial. Thus, a description of two things, A and B, that change their relative positions in space, would be this:

At time$_1$ A is north of B.
At time$_2$ A is south of B.

Therefore, a description of two things, A and B, that change their positions in time, would be nothing other than this:

At place$_1$ A is future to B.
At place$_2$ A is past to B.

And, in fact, an example fitting this description is not hard to find. Let A, for example, be a hurricane, occurring gradually over an area that includes two towns, and let B be a stroke of a clock, any place in the world. It is perfectly possible that in one town A is future to B, and in the other, past to B, which fulfills the description. Of course there is a temptation here, again, to think of the hurricane as really consisting of many events, such that what happens in one town is different from what happens in the other. But this only calls attention to the fact that an interval of space is required to make the example work, or in other words, that there must be two places given, and the hurricane must exist at both of them. We have, however, already seen that an interval of time is absolutely required for something to change its spatial position, or in other words, that there must be two times given, and that the thing in question must exist at both of them. The analogy is, therefore, complete.

Such comparisons as those we have suggested can sometimes be worked out with astonishing results, though they are apt to become somewhat complex and put a strain on the mind. If, for example, one renders an exact description of an object that *changes places* with another in space, or of one that *approaches* another and then *recedes* from it, he will find that he can also render an exact description of an object that changes places with another in time, or of one that approaches another in time and then recedes from it. One need only make the descriptions complete and identical in both cases, except that all spatial relations are replaced by temporal ones, and vice versa. The one thing that must be borne in mind, however, is that whenever one allows for a lapse of time in one description, he must also allow for a lapse of space in the other. If, for instance, a lapse of time is needed for two objects to change places in space, as of course it is, then a lapse of space must be allowed for in the description of two objects that change places in time.

CHAPTER EIGHT

The Relativity
of Time and Space

Most people think of time as a great river. This gives rise to much confusion, the commonest being, as we have seen, the idea of getting into a "time machine" and "going back" or perhaps even "going forth" in time, as one might get into a boat and go up or down a river.

Thus time is thought of as something that flows, like a river, at a constant rate and in one direction only. A river wears down the things in its path, and things similarly age and decay over time. A river has a distant and obscure source, and eventually flows into a vast ocean. Philosophers and theologians have similarly speculated on the beginning of time itself, and on the vast and unflowing eternity in which it ends.

Space, on the other hand, is popularly thought of as resembling not a river but a great and motionless vessel within which everything is spread out and contained. Thus we think of objects as moving through space, much as fish move about in a vast lake.

The fundamental error in these popular conceptions is thinking of time and space as *things* or, in Kantian terms, as "real beings." Space and time are not things. The words derive their meaning from certain relationships that all objects have to each other. Examples of common *spatial* relationships, for example, are those of being next to, being distant from, approaching, receding, surrounding, being inside of or outside of, and so on. Similarly, familiar *temporal* relationships are those of being simultaneous with, being earlier or later than, being younger or older than, being brief or persisting, and so on.

TIME AND MOTION

The concept of time is inseparable from the concept of change. When one thinks of "the passage of time" one is likely to think of sand flowing in an hour glass, the lengthening shadow of a sun dial, or of aging. And it is, of course, from the regularly changing relationships of the earth, moon, and sun that our basic temporal concepts arise. A *day* is the "amount of time" required for one rotation of the earth. But that is misleadingly expressed. We should say, rather, that "one day" refers to the temporal distance between adjacent sunrises. The term "year" similarly refers to the temporal distance between, for example, adjacent winter solstices. And the idea of a month derives from the regular but ever changing relationship between earth and moon.

These three concepts — day, year, and month — are not purely conventional, for they rest upon unalterable natural cycles. Thus we could not, for example, divide a year into one hundred days, the way we have divided days into twenty-four hours rather than, say, twenty. Clocks could be designed to complete their regular cycles twenty times per day, rather than twenty-four, and this would not generate any real problems of time measurement. But a year cannot be thus arbitrarily divided up.

All temporal relationships are set against the background, not of some great river of time, but rather, the orderly and repetitive configurations of earth, sun, and moon. To enable us to refer to events, and when they occur, and how they are related to others, we arbitrarily designate one such set of configurations as a point of departure. Thus, "year one" refers to that set of configurations of sun, earth, and moon that coincide with some more or less dramatic event, such as the birth of some religious figure. Then, given that framework, *any* event, large or small, can be located within it, and the events then related to each other, as being before or after, and the extent of their temporal separation can be measured. Thus we can locate great and complex events, such as the rise and fall of nations, or small and simple ones, such as the winning of a race, where a fraction of a second becomes crucial. But in all such cases we are relating events to the successive configurations of earth, sun, and moon, or, more generally, to the earth in relation to the heavens; nothing more.

PARTICULAR TIMES

Inasmuch as time, considered as an endless, invisible, and intangible thing perpetually flowing upon us, has no real being, the same must be true of particular times, even though philosophers and others often allude to times as if pointing to identifiable things.

The corresponding point can perhaps be more readily seen with respect to individual places. Thus, if you allude to particular places, by such expressions as "Times Square," "the finish line," "where we met," and so on, you find that you are in fact only referring to physical objects, which are located not by the places they somehow occupy but by their spatial relationships to other objects. Spatial locations are, accordingly, purely relative. Thus one might toss his hat into the back seat of his car, spend the day driving around, and then say that the hat was right there, in the same place, the whole time. The statement is true, or false, depending on what other objects are being indirectly referred to as reference frames.

It is the same with times. Thus, such expressions as "the time of Socrates' birth," "the moment the race began," "the Elizabethan era," and so on — all of which appear to refer to particular times, of greater or lesser duration — really refer only to things and events in relation to other things and events. "The moment the race began," for example, does not refer to some bit of time, but to some such set of events as the firing of a gun, the state of a clock, and, ultimately, the temporal relationships of these to earth and sun. Thus time is, like space, relative.

TEMPORAL DIRECTION

We think of time as having a fixed direction, like an arrow that cannot be turned around or, again, a river that cannot be reversed. The future is something necessarily lying ahead of us, and the past, behind us.

The ascription of temporal direction rests, however, not on any metaphysical feature of time, but on the irreversibility of certain processes, that is, changes in objects. Some changes have no such fixed sequence. Thus one can design a clock that runs backwards. Ice can melt, then refreeze, and melt again. You can walk to the store, then walk home again, even walking backwards if you have the patience. Other changes, however, have a fixed and unalterable direction. Thus a fried egg cannot become unfried and restored to its shell. Light emanates from a candle flame, but the reverse process is impossible. An acorn grows to an oak, but never the reverse. Other examples of such irreversibility come easily to mind. The general description of any such process is that it contains a set of states, namely, A, B, C . . . etc., which are such that, as a matter of physical law, A must precede B, B must precede C, and so on, the reverse sequence being impossible. Thus, the alleged "direction of time" turns out to be a feature only of some, but not all, temporal processes, that is, relations between states of things. If every process were reversible, then there would be nothing to suggest any inherent direction of time.

CHAPTER NINE

Temporal Passage

One thing concerning time that has always been the greatest stumbling block to comparing it with space is its *passage* or *flow,* or what amounts to the same thing, the characteristic all things seem to have of continuously moving along through time. Thus, we speak of future things as *drawing nearer,* of then *becoming* present and, having passed into the present, of *receding* endlessly into an ever-growing past. These are all expressions of change or movement. They clearly imply that something is moving, though certainly not in the ordinary manner in which things move. In fact, something needs only to be in time, or in other words, to exist as an object, in order to be moving in the manner suggested; for concerning any such object we can say that, until it exists, it draws closer and closer to existing; that while it exists it becomes older; and after it ceases to exist it recedes ever farther into the past.

This kind of motion or passage, which seems to be such a basic and even necessary characteristic of time, has profoundly bewildered philosophers ever since St. Augustine tried, without much success, to make sense of it in his *Confessions.* It becomes so strange and loaded with absurdities, as soon as one tries to think rationally about it, that some thinkers have simply concluded that it is an illusion and that, accordingly, time itself must be unreal. Plato, taking this view, called time nothing but a moving image of eternity, the suggestion being that what is only an image has no genuine reality, but that eternity does. Eternity is the realm of reality in which there is no change, becoming, or decay. It has been almost characteristic of metaphysics to take this view. Eternity is the temporal dimension of the world as it would be seen by an eternal and changeless being such as God. Nothing arises or perishes, as thus apprehended; it simply *is*. There is here no becoming or changing, no growing older. Concerning the universe and all it contains, one can say that it exists. One cannot in addition say that it is passing through time, or that time is passing over it.

For example, one can say, concerning some more or less interesting thing, such as your birth, that there is such an event. And one can say concerning another more or less interesting thing, such as your death, that there is also such an event as that. Further, one can say that the first of these is *earlier* than the other, and that there are other events in the world — such as the birth of your father — to which it is subsequent; and that there are other events with which it is simultaneous. And so it is with everything that ever exists or happens. The entire universe is spread out in a changeless space and a changeless time, and everything in it has a place, defined by its spatial relationships to other things, and a time, defined by its temporal relationships to other things. Things move in space, in the sense that something can be at one place at one time and at another place at another time, but there is no sense in which space itself can be described as moving. Similarly, as we have seen, things move in time, in the sense that something can be at one time at one place and at another time at another place, but there is no sense in which time itself can be described as moving. Or at least, that is the view of things that a metaphysical mind is apt to prefer.

Still, it cannot be denied that things in time *seem* to pass into, through, and out of existence. That can be our datum or starting point, and if metaphysics declares this to be an illusion, then it is up to metaphysics to show it is. Until the illusory character of this apprehension has been demonstrated, then we can say, concerning anything whatever that ever exists, that until it exists it draws ever closer to existing; that while it exists it grows older; and that after it ceases to exist it recedes ever farther into the past. Or at least, so it certainly seems.

Conscious and reflective beings like us find the passage of time inescapable. No metaphysical theories can make this passage seem less real to us who dwell in time and who look forward and back in it. Past things have a sense of distance quite unlike things that are present, and the recession of things past is something that can almost be felt. We sometimes want to grasp for them, to seize them, and hold them a bit longer, but this in vain. Human beings have both the inherent determination to exist and the intelligence or understanding to realize that their tenure of existence is limited. One's passage through time is for oneself, then, an appalling fact. That lifeless things should deteriorate and perish makes no difference anywhere. These things have no will to life and no dread of its passage and cessation. The fact that their duration is finite has no more significance than that their bulk is such. If the world turned lifelessly around, carrying only its atmosphere and lifeless things upon it, its passage through time would be quite without significance, and it would not matter whether it was now turning for the millionth or the thousand millionth time. But a person is aware that his life is something that he *passes through*, and that its end is something that, whether near or remote, is nonetheless surely *approaching*. Whether it is his thousandth or twenty thousandth sunrise that he is seeing makes an overwhelming difference, for it marks the extent of his pilgrimage along a path upon which he can neither pause nor turn back, and that has only one possible destination, which is the cessation of his own being. It marks, in fact, how much is gone, and how much is still left, of his own ebbing existence. Nor is it here the mere prospect of his debility that appalls, for a man would be only partially comforted by the realization that the vigor of his youth could be held a bit longer. It is the fact of *passage* itself, with or without the vigor of youth, that concerns one. Someone awaiting certain execution draws no comfort from the fact that he need suffer no decay before death. It is the approach of the latter by itself, and the total calamity of it, that voids his hope. It is perhaps worth noting, however, that every one of us is approaching his end, no less certainly and inevitably than one who has had its date fixed for him.

PURE BECOMING

Let us use the expression "pure becoming" to designate the passage through time to which all things seem to be subjected, merely by virtue of their being in time. It is aptly called *pure* becoming because any other kind of change or becoming that anything might undergo *presupposes* this kind of change, whereas this pure becoming presupposes no other change at all. Thus, in order for anything to become red, or square, or larger, or weaker, or whatnot, it must pass through a certain amount of time, which is equivalent to saying that it must *become older*. The fact that something becomes older, however, or that it acquires a greater age than it had does not entail that it undergoes any other change whatever.

The idea of a thing's becoming older is not always, to be sure, thought of in this metaphysical sense. When we describe something as becoming older we often have in mind certain definite and observable changes. For instance, if we say of a man that he is becoming older, we are apt to be referring to the diminution of his strength or vigor, and so on. Aging is, in this sense, simply a physiological concept, and as it is used in this way we can speak without absurdity of someone's aging more or less rapidly, or even of his becoming younger.

By *pure becoming*, however, we have in mind becoming older simply in the sense of acquiring a greater age, whether that increase of age is attended by any other changes or not. In this sense a thing can become older without undergoing any other change whatever, for it can simply increase in age from one day to the next. This, then, seems to be a kind of becoming or passing through time that can be asserted of anything whatever that exists in time, for it is a consequence simply of its being in time. A thing can be as stable and unchanging as we care to suppose, and yet this appears to be one change that nothing can elude. Even if something should acquire the attributes of newness, and thus elude the process of aging in that sense, it would still have to become older to do so. If a decaying flower, for instance, resumed the fresh form of a bud, it would in one sense appear to become younger but it would nonetheless become older, for otherwise no meaning could be given to the idea of its *resuming* that form. We could say of such a flower on any given day, whatever might be its form and properties, that it is a day older than it was yesterday, that in the meantime it has *become* older, however new and young it may seem. And this, of course, would mark a change — namely, a change in its age, which it had in time undergone.

Now, for anything to be passing through time or becoming older it must, of course, exist. Nonentities do not become older or pass through time, for they are not even *in* time; nor do real things that once existed but have since ceased, or other real things that will at some time exist but that do not exist yet. Diogenes' cup, for instance, became both old and rusty, but both changes ceased with the cessation of that cup's existence. Yet even things that have ceased to exist, and others that will exist in the future but do not exist yet, undergo a *relational* kind of change that is simply a corollary of pure becoming or passage through time. That is, we can speak of Diogenes' cup as *receding* ever farther into the past. It is more remote from us in time today than it was yesterday, and this is a relational change it is undergoing. Similarly, the birth of my first grandchild, assuming there will be one, is something that is *drawing closer*, and this is a relational change that something that will, but does not yet, exist, is already undergoing. I can look forward to it now, but someday I shall only be able to look back upon it; and this is a change that it will meanwhile have undergone and is even now undergoing, in relation to me. Nor is this merely a change in the manner in which I choose to view it, for it is no matter of my choice at all. Just as I cannot now look forward in anticipation to using Diogenes' cup, because this has forever after — for all future time — ceased to be, so also I cannot now look back in memory to the birth of my first grandchild, because this has forever before — for all past time — not yet come to be.

THE STRANGENESS OF THIS IDEA

This kind of passage or change is surely very odd, so odd that anyone who thinks about it is apt to feel impelled either to deny outright that it even exists, which amounts to denying the datum with which we began, or else to find alternative ways of expressing it. The idea of pure becoming or temporal passage will seem even more strange, however, in the light of the following considerations.

In the first place, we must note that pure becoming is not only an unobservable change but is compatible with, and in fact entailed by, any change whatever that is observed. If, for instance, we see that something, such as a leaf, is green and then becomes red, or red and then becomes green, we must conclude that it also becomes older, for nothing can become anything at all without becoming older in the process. The conception of something's becoming older, then, is a purely *a priori* notion, a consequence of its simply being in time. Second, any event is a change, and it is therefore quite odd to think of events as themselves changing. Yet events are in time and have duration; hence, while they last, they become older, and when they have ceased they begin an endless recession into the past, like anything else. And finally, the continual recession of things past, and the advance upon us of things future, is a strange kind of passage for the reason that no *rate* of passage can possibly be assigned to it without making nonsense. We cannot, for instance, sensibly say that Diogenes' cup is receding into the past at the rate of one day every twenty-four hours, or even at the rate of one day for every complete rotation of the earth; but what else can one say?

Confronted with such considerations as these, it is tempting to dismiss the pure becoming or temporal passage of things as an illusion, to say that nothing ever really does change in this sense. If a metaphysician wants to make a case for this, he has abundant materials with which to construct his arguments. This amounts, however, to denying the datum with which we began. Moreover, in case the idea of the passage or flow of time is essential to the very conception of time itself, as it may well be, then to deny that there is any such passage would amount to denying that anything is even in time at all. Ever so many metaphysicians have found this conclusion an agreeable one, but it is hardly in accordance with one of the most basic convictions of mankind. However puzzling it may be to metaphysics, it is very difficult for anyone really to convince himself of the falseness of the idea that the end of his life, for example, whether it be near or remote, is something that is approaching, that it will, alas, become present, and that it will then begin receding into the past. Such a statement is readily understood by everyone and seems quite certainly to express a fact of some sort. If a prisoner who is awaiting execution is told that the hour of his death is approaching and already near, he realizes that he has learned something of great importance to himself. He knows that there is little left of his life, and that what little is left is diminishing with every passing moment. His terror at this thought would hardly be relieved by his having it pointed out to him by a metaphysician that this kind of change is very strange and even absurd. However strange and mysterious the passage of time might be, it is sometimes nonetheless appalling.

TIME AND A RIVER

While temporal passage is a difficult philosophical concept, it should not be compared with the flow of a river. A river flows at a certain rate — for example, two miles per hour — but, as we have noted, no rate can be assigned to the passage of time. To say that time passes at a "rate" of one day at a time is no more meaningful than saying it passes one year at a time, nor can any meaning be given here to the words "at a time." Similarly, to speak of "one day every twenty-four hours" is merely to signify that a day can be thus divided into hours, just as a foot can be divided into inches. This is not of philosophical interest.

Again, the flow of a river can be stopped, or sometimes accelerated, or retarded, by dams, for instance; but no meaning can be given to time stopping, speeding up, or slowing. When people speak of time "standing still" what they actually imagine is everything *but* time standing still. They imagine a total cessation of all change — for a certain brief or long *period of time.* Similarly, when one tries to form an idea of time moving more or less rapidly, he finds himself imagining something other than time increasing or decreasing its rate of change. If, for example, a man were to pass from birth to adolescence, maturity, old age, and death all in a single year, then this would not mean that time had, for him, been greatly accelerated. It would mean, rather, that his life processes had been accelerated. All the stages of his life are imagined to occur within the fixed time of one standard year.

THE ELUSIVE PRESENT

The words "time" and "space," we have noted, are not names of things, and hence do not stand for strange beings that flow, expand, contract, or do anything at all. Instead, then, of speaking of time and space, we should speak of temporal and spatial relationships between things. And the temporal relationships between things and events, it should now be noted, do not change. If a given event occurs one hour before another, then that always was and always will be the temporal relationship the two events have to each other. Viewing the matter this way, then the whole history of the world, together with its entire future, can be regarded as fixed and changeless, for the relationship which any event whatever has to every other event that ever occurs, whether past, present, or future, is quite unalterable. Thus your birth and your death, two events that are of momentous importance to you, are eternally separated by a certain fixed interval of time, which is the length of your life, and this never changes.

The pastness or futurity of an event, however, is not something that is fixed and unchanging. We are especially aware of this with respect to all those things we view as being *present.* They seem to be continuously slipping away.

We feel this more and more acutely as we get older, for what is left of our lives seems to be constantly shrinking, just as what has already been lived seems to be constantly growing. Perhaps this is why old people dwell so much on the past, but give little thought to the future. The former has become rich and full, while the latter seems to be rapidly, and depressingly, dwindling to nothingness.

The philosophical problem of temporal passage, or what has been called "pure becoming," can be expressed by saying that, when a given set of events or items of history have been completely described in terms of which ones come before and which ones come after some other event or set of events, we still do not know which, if any, are past and which future. For example, consider the set of lunar eclipses visible from a certain place over a period of one hundred years. Call these A, B, C . . . etc., with the understanding that A occurs before B, that B occurs before C, and so on, and let the temporal distances, or "amounts of time," between them be specified. Now we still do not know, from such a description, which of these events, if any, have already occurred, and which, if any, are still in the future. These properties, moreover, seem to be changing ones, for if any of these events happens to be a future one, then it will eventually cease to be future, briefly become present, and then, it would seem, commence its endless recession into the past. And this seems inconsistent with the conception of time endorsed by most philosophers, to the effect that all statements involving time can be reduced to statements describing the temporal relationships of events to each other.

One way of trying to get around this difficulty is to understand "the present" as referring not to some fleeting moment, but rather to a certain changeless date, and then treat the events under consideration as occurring either before or after that date. Thus, the statement that a lunar eclipse occurs on July 3, 1989, will turn out to be equivalent to saying that it is future, on every date prior to then, and that it is past on every date thereafter.

This proposed solution does not work, however, for even though the date of the event is understood, one still does not know whether that event is occurring now, is going to occur, or has already occurred, unless he *also* happens to know which date happens to correspond with the present moment. And that is something that changes. The date itself is something that is at one time future, then becomes present, and shortly thereafter slips into the past, and we thus still have on our hands the same problem with which we began.

Suppose, then, we try relating such a set of events, not to some fleeting present moment, but to the very act of describing or alluding to them, which is of course nothing but an additional event. Thus, we can understand the description "the eclipse that is occurring now," to be a reference to whatever eclipse happens to coincide with the utterance of that very description. And this, of course, amounts to nothing more than asserting the simultaneity of two events. To say that a given pair of events occur simultaneously implies nothing about any mysterious kind of temporal passage

This proposal contains the same difficulty as the preceding one, however, for we can now ask whether the utterance alluded to is one that is occurring *now*, or whether it is one that is past, perhaps long past. The mere assertion of the coincidence of an eclipse with someone's description of it tells us nothing about when the eclipse occurs, unless we know when, in relation to the fleeting present, that description occurs.

So finally, approaching the problem from still another direction, let us suppose that the idea of the *present* is not really a temporal concept at all, but rather, a psychological one, referring, not to some elusive moment of time, but to what William James and others have called "the specious present." Thus, in speaking of an event as happening *now*, one simply relates the event in question to his awareness of it.

But here, not surprisingly, the same problem recurs, for one can now ask, concerning the state of awareness alluded to, whether it is one's *present* awareness, or perhaps some past awareness that is now merely being recalled. And with that it can be seen that we have made no progress at all with respect to getting rid of the concept of the present moment and its elusive character.

Thus the passage of time seems to remain as an irreducible mystery — not mysterious in the sense of being unknown, for nothing could be more familiar, but mysterious in the metaphysical sense that it cannot be described in a way that is not an invitation to absurdity. The world would certainly be less philosophically puzzling if all temporal relationships could, like spatial ones, be reduced to relationships between objects. The world could then be thought of as consisting of infinitely many things and events simply spread out in space and time. But the seemingly irreducible mystery of temporal passage, or the fleetingness of the present moment, is a persisting obstacle to such simplicity, and time remains hardly less puzzling than when St. Augustine tried, in vain, to comprehend it.

CHAPTER TEN

Causation

We have already presupposed an understanding of causation in the discussion of determinism, and that presupposition is surely correct. Everyone does understand what causation is. The most untutored, unread person understands what is being said, for example, when told that his neighbor was killed (caused to die) by being kicked in the head by a horse. No amount of metaphysics could enhance his grasp of that fact. Indeed, virtually our entire understanding of what goes on around us consists of the perception of causal connections such as this one. Sometimes the identification of causes in particular cases is difficult and may even take years and the investment of fortunes, but this rarely results from lack of philosophical understanding. One might search for months, for example, for the cause of an airplane crash, but the difficulty here is in verifying the presence of something that answers to the conception of causation we already possess, not in arriving at the conception itself.

What the untutored and vulgar cannot do, however, is put into words what that understanding consists of. And no wonder, for this is enormously hard; the wisest metaphysicians have not to this day been able to agree on how it is to be done. It is not even unreasonable to doubt that it can be done at all. Still, it is worth trying, for hardly any conception could be more basic to metaphysical understanding than this one, or hardly any confusion more mischievous in its philosophical fruits. If a philosopher's analysis of causation goes wrong, then it is a good bet that most of his metaphysics will be wrong too.

What we want, then, is a conceptual analysis of this basic concept we so securely possess. Just what are we asserting when we say that certain things are related as causes and effects?

Here we have to resist the temptation, so beguiling to scholars, to wax learned by drawing our examples from what are, to most, the obscure reaches of science. Nothing is accomplished by this, except to throw an initial darkness over the whole procedure. We want examples that are as clearly understood by the aforesaid uncouth and unread person as by the wisest; for if such an unlearned person can understand them perfectly, they cannot be so difficult of comprehension.

Such statements, then, as "The window was shattered by a brick," "This fire was started by a smoldering cigarette," "A nail punctured that tire," and so on, express causal connections. We would be saying exactly the same things if we said: "A brick caused that window to break," "The fire was caused by a cigarette," and so on.

SUBSTANCES, STATES, AND CHANGES OF STATE

The first thing to note about those statements, like most ordinary statements expressive of causal relations, is that certain objects or substances seem to be referred to as causes — a brick, a cigarette, and a nail. But this is simply a common manner of speaking, and not strictly true. It is not, for example, just the brick *as such* that causes the window to break. It is, rather, the impact of the brick against the window; and this impact is not itself a substance, but a change. This also obtains with respect to the cigarette and the nail. What caused the fire was some flammable thing being raised to the point of ignition by a smoldering cigarette. And the tire was punctured not just by the nail, but by the nail's poking into it. These are *changes* of things, and not things (substances) themselves.

It is equally obvious that, as causes are changes, so are their effects. The fire that was caused, for instance, is not a thing in its own right, but a change in something; namely, whatever it is that is ignited. This is true also with respect to the puncture, which is a change in the condition of the tire, and the shattering, which is a change of state of the glass.

So our first step consists of distinguishing substances, on the one hand, and the state and changes of substances, on the other, and noting that in all typical cause-and-effect situations, the causal connections are between changes or states of substances, and only indirectly between the substances themselves. And the concept of a substance, at least in the present context, need not create any special difficulties. We can define it, for the present purpose, as anything that can be poked with a stick — a cigarette, a tire, a nail, a brick, and so on. States and changes are something quite different, being things that one attributes to or predicates of a substance. These ideas are not hard to grasp, at least at the level required here.

Statements of the form "A caused B," at least in the commonest sense of "caused," are thus usually statements relating certain changes of substances.

What, however, of such a statement of causal connection as "The balloon was kept aloft by hydrogen"? Or "The ice was prevented from melting by its being kept in a freezer"? These are clearly statements of causal connections, and yet what is involved seems not to be changes but rather the absence of changes — the balloon remains aloft, the water remains frozen. But of course what statements like this illustrate is that, as *changes* of state can be related as causes and effects, so can *persistences* of state. Changes are sometimes prevented, as well as produced, and in either case causation is involved. In the case of the balloon, it is the state of its content, hydrogen, being lighter than air, that accounts for another state, that of the balloon remaining aloft. Similarly, for the ice — it remains frozen because it remains cold, and these are both unchanging states.

We can now tie these preliminary considerations together as follows: We begin with an ordinary object or thing; that is with a *substance* — a brick, window, tire, or nail — and distinguish it from its *states* — the state of being hard, red, in motion, sharp, warm, and so forth. A *change* of any substance is its transition from one state to another — it becomes soft, dull, cold, green, stationary, or whatever. *Causes* are always states or, more typically, changes, and so likewise are *effects*; that is, certain changes of state cause certain others, and in some cases certain persisting states are the causes of the persistence of certain others. The *cause-and-effect relationship*, therefore, is a relationship between changes of state or, sometimes, persistences of state, and only indirectly is it a relationship between the substances themselves to which those states belong.

THE NECESSARY CONNECTION OF CAUSES
TO THEIR EFFECTS

We now address ourselves to this metaphysical question: What is the relationship between changes or states of substances such that some can be described as the causes, or the effects, of others?

Historically, the main dispute over this question has been whether or not that relationship involves any *necessitation* of effects by their causes, or whether it is merely the *de facto* relationship of joint occurrence. Do causes compel the occurrence of their effects? Is there any necessary connection between them? Or do certain effects invariably, though not necessarily, follow upon certain causes? Would there be any rational absurdity involved in the conception of familiar changes being followed by effects radically different from those to which we are accustomed? Might water, for example, be ignited instead of solidified by chilling? Or glass rendered stronger by being struck by a brick? Or fires extinguished by having gasoline put on them? Such things never happen. But is that the whole truth of the matter? Or shall we say that they *cannot* happen? That it is impossible, there being a necessary connection between those causes with which we are familiar and their accustomed effects?

It is an interesting and fundamental question, and the reason it has divided philosophers so long seems to be that the dispute has been carried on in the spirit of ideology and debate. Partisans of the more metaphysical view, that there is a connection of necessity between certain changes and states, have to some extent tried to win acceptance of their opinion simply by emphatic reiteration of it ("When the club hits the ball, the ball just *has* to move," etc.), while those of the opposite persuasion have adduced numberless irrelevancies, such as pointing out that no such necessary connection is observable, that the empirical sciences presuppose no such idea, and so on.

There is, however, no need to adduce dubious pros and cons, for there is a fairly straightforward *test* of the various claims that have been made as alternatives to the metaphysical theory of a necessary connection. The test is simply to consider any particular analysis of the causal relationship that explicitly *omits* any reference to a necessary connection between cause and effect, and then see whether an example can be contrived wherein certain changes or states are related in precisely the manner described in that analysis, but that are nevertheless *not* related as cause and effect. This mode of refutation is called "the counter-example." It is, of course, frightfully effective and, indeed, decisive.

Let us, then, use capital letters, A, B, C, . . . etc., to designate actual changes or states of actual substances, and consider some typical and *true* statement of the form "A was the cause of B." Let A, for example, be the rubbing of a certain match against a rough surface in a certain way, and B its igniting immediately thereafter. But note that these are to be considered actual changes that in fact occur at a certain time and place and in a certain way, not changes that might occur at this time or that or in any of various ways, or kinds of changes. And note, too, that the statement in question must be considered true; that is, we are talking about an actual match that was caused to ignite by its being rubbed in a certain way. Our question, then, is not: Is there a causal connection here? Nor: How do we know there is a causal connection here? But rather: Assuming that A was the cause of B, and that this is known, what does it *mean* to say that?

CONSTANT CONJUNCTION

Does it, for example, mean merely that A and B are constantly conjoined in our experience, B always following upon A? Plainly not, for the change designated by A, as well as that designated by B, occurred only once in the history of the universe. The statement, then, that A and B are "constantly" conjoined is true enough — whenever A occurs, B occurs — but it is a trivial truth. Any two changes that jointly occur are, whether causally related or not, "constantly" conjoined, since each occurs only once.

Here there is, of course, a great temptation to introduce the idea of similarity, and to say that A was the cause of B, provided A was immediately followed by B, and that things similar to A are, in similar circumstances, always followed by things similar to B — for example, that when matches similar to a given one are treated in a similar way, there is a similar result.

This is very beguiling, not because the philosophical difficulty has been overcome, but rather because it has been concealed. For what does "similar" mean in this context? If we take it to mean *exact* similarity, then we find that there is only one thing on earth exactly similar to A, namely A itself and likewise, only one thing exactly similar to B. The statement, then, that things similar to A are in similar circumstances "always" followed by things similar to B becomes trivial, A and B themselves being the only two things in the universe having the requisite similarity. Other things are only more or less similar to these — similar, that is, in some respects, but dissimilar in others.

If, however, we allow this similarity to be a matter of degree, no longer requiring that it be exact, then the statement that things similar to A are in similar circumstances always followed by things similar to B is no longer true. It therefore cannot constitute an analysis of the *true* statement that A was the cause of B. A clay imitation match, for example, is rather similar to the real one but it does not ignite when rubbed; this is also true in the case of a wet match. Even a real match, when rubbed on a smooth surface, is apt not to ignite — though a smooth surface is more or less similar to the rough one we were considering. It may be of the same shape and color, for example. And even, for that matter, real matches do not *always* ignite, even when rubbed on surfaces exactly like the one we are considering. Hence, the claim that in similar circumstances similar things respond to similar changes in similar ways is really not true, if the similarity is merely one of degree. Things quite similar sometimes behave entirely differently.

At this point, of course, one wants to introduce the idea of relevance and say that things that are *in relevant respects* similar to A respond, in relevantly similar circumstances, in ways similar to B. This, however, just gives the whole thing away, for it at once becomes obvious that "relevant respects" are nothing other than those features of the situation that are causally related. Suppose, for instance, we have two pairs of matches. The first two are similar to each other in all respects, except that one is wet and the other dry. The other two are likewise similar in all respects, except that one is red and the other blue. Now, the *degree* of similarity within each pair is exactly the same, each match differing from its mate in only one respect. One of the differences is a relevant one, however, while the other is not. Whether a match is red or blue is irrelevant to the question of whether or not it ignites when rubbed in a certain way; it does not matter what color it is. But whether it is wet or dry is not irrelevant; it makes all the difference in the world. All this means, however, is that the dryness of a match is *causally connected* with its igniting, while its color is not. The introduction of the idea of relevant similarity has therefore been useless, as far as providing any kind of philosophical analysis of causation is concerned. It already incorporates the idea of causation.

LAWS OF NATURE

Sometimes difficulties of the kind just considered have been countered by introducing the idea of a law of nature into the description of causal connections. Thus, one might say that a given change A was the cause of another, B, provided there is a law to the effect that every change that resembles A in certain specified respects is always accompanied or followed by another that resembles B in certain specified respects. It is, for example, a law of nature that zinc always dissolves in sulphuric acid, given certain specifiable conditions of temperature, etc. This appears to express a causal connection, but without any reference to necessity. The law does not say that zinc *must* behave that way, but only that it always does.

This appeal to laws does not work, however, if it is thought to eliminate the idea of necessity, for that idea is still there, though hidden. A general statement of the kind considered counts as the expression of a law only if one can use it to infer not only what does or will happen but also what would happen if something else, which does not happen, were to happen. Thus, one can say of a given lump of zinc that, let us suppose, never has and never will come in contact with sulphuric acid, that if it *were* to be placed in that liquid under certain easily specifiable conditions, it *would* dissolve. And this statement obviously says more, or is a stronger statement, than any statement of what merely *does* happen, or even what always happens.

Let us clarify this with another example. Consider a true and perfectly general statement to the effect that any match having a certain specified set of properties ignites when rubbed in a certain specified manner under specified conditions. Suppose, for example, we took a quantity of matches — a thousand, say — and gave them a common set of properties that uniquely distinguished them from every match that ever has or ever will exist. We can suppose, for example, that we decorate the sticks with a certain unusual pattern, so that each of these matches resembles each of the others with respect to that pattern, but, we are supposing, does not, in that respect, resemble any other match that ever has or ever will exist, since no other match will ever be so decorated. (It is not relevant, at this point, to ask how this might be known. It does not matter.) Now if each of those thousand matches, thus decorated, were rubbed in a certain way — against a fresh piece of sandpaper, let us suppose — it might be true that *every* match (in the history of the universe) having those properties ignites when rubbed in that manner. But this would be no law of nature, even though it would then be a true and perfectly general statement asserting how certain things, all resembling one another in certain precisely described ways, invariably behave under certain precisely described conditions, admitting of not a single exception in the history of the universe. The reason it would be no law is that there is no necessary connection between those particular properties — the pattern on the match sticks — and the way the matches behave when rubbed. If, contrary to fact, another match *were* to have those properties but lacked, let us say, the property of dryness (not mentioned in our general statement), it might not ignite. For a true general statement of this kind to count as a law of nature, then, we must be able to use it to infer what would happen if something else, which does not happen, were to happen. But this expresses a necessary and not a merely *de facto* connection between certain changes and states. Common sense expresses this by saying, quite rightly, that there is some connection between a match's being dry and igniting when rubbed, but no connection between its being decorated in a certain way and igniting when it is rubbed. But this means only that the decoration has nothing to do with, or no necessary connection with, a match's igniting when rubbed, while its being dry does.

Here one might be tempted to point out that it is, after all, only by experience that causal connections are discovered. We have to see what changes and states are invariably conjoined. We do not see any necessary connection between them, or anything about any given change or property from which we can infer that it *must* be followed by whatever does follow it. We only observe that it is.

But this observation, so familiar to philosophy, whether it is true or not, has no relevance to the question before us. The question is not how causes are known, but rather what they are. We began by assuming that we know, at least in some instances, that certain things are causally connected. The most untutored person knows this. *How* these connections are known is an interesting question, but not the question we are asking. Our question is rather what one *means* when he affirms the existence of a connection that is thus so confidently known.

CAUSES AS NECESSARY
AND SUFFICIENT CONDITIONS

In the light of all the foregoing we can now set forth our problem as follows: Every change occurs under innumerable and infinitely complex conditions. Some of these are relevant to the occurrence of the change in question, others have nothing to do with it. This means that some of those conditions are such that the change would not have occurred without them, and the rest had nothing to do with it.

Consider again, for example, the particular change consisting of a given match igniting at a certain time and place, and assume that this was caused.

Now it would be impossible to set forth all the conditions under which this occurred, for they were numberless. A complete description of them would be a
description of the entire universe in every detail. Nevertheless, we can suppose that there were, among those innumerable conditions, the following: (1)
the state consisting of the match's being dry, (2) the change consisting of its
being rubbed in a certain way, (3) its being of such-and-such chemical composition, (4) the rubbing surface being of such-and-such roughness, (5) the presence of dust particles in the air nearby, (6) the sun shining, (7) the presence of
an observer named Smith, and so on. Now some of those conditions —
namely, (1) through (4), and others not mentioned — had something causally
to do with the match igniting, while others — (5), for instance — probably
had no causal connection with that change. Our problem, then, is to state not
how we know this but rather, just what relationship those causal conditions
had to the match's igniting that the other conditions had not.

The most natural thing to say is that, had conditions (1) through (4) not occurred, the match would not have ignited, and the remaining conditions, (5)
through (7), made no difference. This, however, is simply a way of saying that
the former were *necessary conditions* for the occurrence of the change in question (the ignition of the match), and the latter were not.

If this is correct then we can tentatively define causation as follows: *The
cause, A, of any change (or persisting state), B, is that totality of conditions from
among all those, but only those, that occurred, each of which was necessary for the
occurrence (or persistence) of B.*

If, moreover, the set of conditions designated A is taken, as it should be, to
include *every* condition that occurred and was necessary for B, such that no
others were necessary, then we can say that the set of conditions, A, was also
sufficient for B, or such that, given A, B could not have failed to occur.

We can, accordingly, now understand the relationship between any set of
conditions (changes and states) A, and any set of conditions B, expressed in
the statement that *A was the cause of B,* to be clearly and tersely described in
this way: *That A was the set of conditions, from among all those that occurred,
each of which was necessary, and the totality of which was sufficient, for the occurrence of B.*

The terms "necessary" and "sufficient" are of course correlates, and each
can be defined in terms of the concept of impossibility in this way: To say that
A was *necessary* for B means that B would have been impossible given the nonoccurrence of A; and to say that A was *sufficient* for B means that the nonoccurrence of B would have been impossible given A.

CAUSAL NECESSITY

It is obvious that this analysis of causation involves the notion of necessity that
so many philosophers have been eager to banish. To say of any condition that

a given change would not have occurred without it is exactly the same as saying of that condition that it was *necessary* for the occurrence of the change in question. There seems, however, to be no other way of distinguishing the causal conditions for the occurrence of any given event from those innumerable other conditions that are present, but have nothing to do with its occurrence. It should, however, be noted that "necessary" does not in this context mean *logically* necessary, such that it would be a contradiction in terms to say that the change in question occurred in the absence of some condition described as necessary for it. Those who have insisted that there is no logical connection between causes and effects have doubtless spoken correctly, or at least the claim need not be argued here. It is perhaps not *logically* impossible that a given match should ignite from no cause at all. Still, we can sometimes affirm of a given match that it would not have ignited had it not been rubbed, which is to assert a necessary, though not a logically necessary, connection between the two changes.

The analysis thus far given does not, to be sure, express a certain very common conception of what a cause is, but that is only because common usage is sometimes imprecise. Most people, that is, think of the cause of some change as some *one* condition that is conspicuous, novel, or, most likely, within someone's control. In the illustration we have been using, for example, the friction on the match would ordinarily be thought of as "the cause" of its igniting, without regard to its dryness, its chemical composition, and so on. But the reason for this, obviously, is that these other conditions are taken for granted. They are not mentioned, not because they are thought to have no causal connection with the match's igniting, but because they are presupposed. Philosophically it makes no difference whether we say that (1) given the other conditions necessary for the match's igniting, it was then caused to ignite by being rubbed, or that (2) its being rubbed was, together with these other necessary conditions, the cause of its igniting. Its being rubbed has neither more nor less to do with its igniting than does, say, its being dry. The only difference is that it was presumably dry all the while and, in that state, was rubbed.

NECESSITY AS INDISPENSABILITY

Another clarification required at this point arises from the consideration that there is a sense in which no particular condition is ever really necessary for the occurrence of any particular change, nor is any particular set of such conditions ever really sufficient for such a change. From this it would follow, absurdly, that on the analysis given, changes do not have any causes.

A match's being rubbed, for example, does not seem necessary for its igniting, such that it cannot ignite without being rubbed. There are other ways to ignite matches — by touching them to hot surfaces, for example. Moreover, the totality of supposed necessary conditions may not be sufficient for its igniting, since the match could be prevented from igniting, even if all those conditions were present — by suddenly soaking it with water, for example.

This kind of objection is ill considered, however, for it overlooks an essential element of the analysis. It was claimed that the cause of a given change B was that set of conditions that were, *within the totality of those other conditions, and only those, that in fact occurred*, individually necessary and jointly sufficient for B. If, in terms of our example, that totality of other conditions that actually occurred did not, in fact, include some such condition as the match's being in contact with a hot surface, or becoming soaked with water, and so on, then within the totality of all the conditions that *did* occur, its being rubbed *was* necessary for its igniting, and was also, together with certain other conditions that occurred, sufficient for this.

CAUSATION AND TIME

Effects cannot precede their causes in time. This seems never to be doubted, though the metaphysical explanation of this is not very obvious. Must they *follow* their causes in time? Or can causes and effects occur contemporaneously?

These seemingly simple questions raise enormous difficulties that, it seems safe to say, philosophers have never quite resolved. The difficulties seem to stem largely from problems concerning the nature of time itself. Some things, however, can be said with some confidence.

The first is that it does not seem essential to the causal relation that effects should come *after* causes in time. Sometimes the two evidently occur simultaneously. In some cases they seem even to begin and end simultaneously. Consider, for example, an engine that is pulling a car down a track. The motion of the engine is surely the cause of the motion of the car, and yet the two are moving along together. The engine does not first move, then pause while the car moves, then move again and wait for the car to catch up. The motion of both objects is perfectly smooth and simultaneous. One might, of course, argue that the engine had to begin moving before the car could move, but it is not clear that this is true, and even if it is, it is irrelevant. What we are considering is a situation in which both are in motion, not that in which the motion was first begun. And in this situation, wherein both are moving, the car being continuously pulled along by the engine, there is no lapse of time between the motion of one and the motion of the other. Moreover, even if we do consider the manner in which this motion was first commenced, it is not even clear there that the engine moved first, and then, after even a brief lapse of time, the car began moving. If the coupling between them is perfectly tight, with no slack whatever, then the very instant the one moves, the other must move too, without delay.

What, then, shall we say? That causes and effects are always, as in this case, contemporaneous? Hardly, for if that were true, there could never be such a thing as a causal chain, or any explanation of any change in terms of antecedent causes. No number of changes, all occurring at the same time, can ever add up to a situation wherein some preceded the others. Yet we do often explain changes in terms of antecedent causes, and quite properly so.

If on the other hand we were to say that effects *always* follow their causes, in time, we would be refuted by the example just considered, that of the engine pulling the car.

What we can say, however, is that effects *follow upon* their causes, understanding this to include cases of the simultaneity of causes and their effects, as well as those of antecedent causation. What the expression does *not* include, of course, is cases of effects preceding their causes.

And this, finally, allows us to define the causal relationship quite exactly as follows: The expression "A was the cause of B" means: *A and B occurred; and A was that set of conditions, among the totality of those that actually occurred, but those only, which was such that each such condition was necessary for the occurrence of B; and the entire set was sufficient for the occurrence of B; and B followed upon A.*

Such is the metaphysics of causation, or at least, the elements of it. The subject is far from easy but, once grasped, it has an enormous capacity to enhance one's understanding of almost everything that falls under the heading of metaphysics.

CHAPTER ELEVEN

God

An active, living, and religious belief in the gods has probably never arisen and been maintained on purely metaphysical grounds. Such beliefs are found in every civilized land and time and are often virtually universal in a particular culture, yet relatively few people have much of a conception of metaphysics. There are in fact entire cultures, such as that of ancient Israel, to whom metaphysics is quite foreign, though these cultures may nevertheless be religious.

Belief in the gods seems to have its roots in human desires and fears, particularly those associated with self-preservation. Like all other creatures, human beings have a profound will to live, which is what mainly gives one's existence a meaning from one sunrise to the next. Unlike other creatures, however, human beings are capable of the full and terrible realization of their own inevitable decay. A person can bring before his mind the image of his own grave, and with it the complete certainty of its ultimate reality, and against this his will naturally recoils. It can hardly seem to him less than an absolute catastrophe, the very end, so far as he is concerned, of everything, though he has no difficulty viewing death, as it touches others more or less remote from himself, as a perhaps puzzling, occasionally distressing, but nonetheless necessary aspect of nature. It is probably partly in response to this fear that human beings turn to the gods, as those beings of such power that they can overturn this verdict of nature.

The sources of religious belief are doubtless much more complex than this, but they seem to lie in the will rather than in speculative intelligence, nevertheless. Those who possess such a belief seldom permit any metaphysical considerations to wrest it from them, while those who lack it are seldom turned toward it by other metaphysical considerations. Still, in every land in which philosophy has flourished, there have been profound thinkers who have sought to discover some metaphysical basis for a rational belief in the existence of some supreme being or beings. Even though religion may properly be a matter of faith rather than reason, still, a philosophical person can hardly help wondering whether it might, at least in part, be also a matter of reason, and whether, in particular, the existence of God might be something that can be not merely believed but shown. It is this question that we want now to consider; that is, we want to see whether there are not strong metaphysical considerations from which the existence of some supreme being might reasonably be inferred.

THE PRINCIPLE OF SUFFICIENT REASON

Suppose you were strolling in the woods and, in addition to the sticks, stones, and other accustomed litter of the forest floor, you one day came upon some quite unaccustomed object, something not quite like what you had ever seen before and would never expect to find in such a place. Suppose, for example, that it is a large ball, about your own height, perfectly smooth and translucent. You would deem this puzzling and mysterious, certainly, but if one considers the matter, it is no more inherently mysterious that such a thing should exist than that anything else should exist. If you were quite accustomed to finding such objects of various sizes around you most of the time, but had never seen an ordinary rock, then upon finding a large rock in the woods one day you would be just as puzzled and mystified. This illustrates the fact that something that is mysterious ceases to seem so simply by its accustomed presence. It is strange indeed, for example, that a world such as ours should exist; yet few people are very often struck by this strangeness but simply take it for granted.

Suppose, then, that you have found this translucent ball and are mystified by it. Now whatever else you might wonder about it, there is one thing you would hardly question; namely, that it did not appear there all by itself, that it owes its existence to something. You might not have the remotest idea whence and how it came to be there, but you would hardly doubt that there was an explanation. The idea that it might have come from nothing at all, that it might exist without there being any explanation of its existence, is one that few people would consider worthy of entertaining.

This illustrates a metaphysical belief that seems to be almost a part of reason itself, even though few ever think upon it; the belief, namely, that there is some explanation for the existence of anything whatever, some reason why it should exist rather than not. The sheer nonexistence of anything, which is not to be confused with the passing out of existence of something, never requires a reason; but existence does. That there should never have been any such ball in the forest does not require any explanation or reason, but that there should ever be such a ball does. If one were to look upon a barren plain and ask why there is not and never has been any large translucent ball there, the natural response would be to ask why there should be; but if one finds such a ball, and wonders why it is there, it is not quite so natural to ask why it should *not* be — as though existence should simply be taken for granted. That anything should not exist, then, and that, for instance, no such ball should exist in the forest, or that there should be no forest for it to occupy, or no continent containing a forest, or no Earth, nor any world at all, do not seem to be things for which there needs to be any explanation or reason; but that such things should be *does* seem to require a reason.

The principle involved here has been called the principle of sufficient reason. Actually, it is a very general principle, and it is best expressed by saying that, in the case of any positive truth, there is some sufficient reason for it, something that, in this sense, makes it true — in short, that there is some sort of explanation, known or unknown, for everything.

Now, some truths depend on something else, and are accordingly called *contingent*, while others depend only upon themselves, that is, are true by their very natures and are accordingly called *necessary*. There is, for example, a reason why the stone on my window sill is warm; namely, that the sun is shining upon it. This happens to be true, but not by its very nature. Hence, it is contingent, and depends upon something other than itself. It is also true that all the points of a circle are equidistant from the center, but this truth depends upon nothing but itself. No matter what happens, nothing can make it false. Similarly, it is a truth, and a necessary one, that if the stone on my window sill is a body, as it is, then it has a form, because this fact depends upon nothing but itself for its confirmation. Untruths are also, of course, either contingent or necessary, it being contingently false, for example, that the stone on my window sill is cold, and necessarily false that it is both a body and formless, because this is by its very nature impossible.

The principle of sufficient reason can be illustrated in various ways, as we have done, and if one thinks about it, he is apt to find that he presupposes it in his thinking about reality, but it cannot be proved. It does not appear to be itself a necessary truth, and at the same time it would be most odd to say it is contingent. If one were to try proving it, he would sooner or later have to appeal to considerations that are less plausible than the principle itself. Indeed, it is hard to see how one could even make an argument for it without already assuming it. For this reason it might properly be called a presupposition of reason itself. One can deny that it is true, without embarrassment or fear of refutation, but one is then apt to find that what he is denying is not really what the principle asserts. We shall, then, treat it here as a datum — not something that is provably true, but as something that people, whether they ever reflect upon it or not, seem more or less to presuppose.

THE EXISTENCE OF A WORLD

It happens to be true that something exists, that there is, for example, a world, and although no one ever seriously supposes that this might not be so, that there might exist nothing at all, there still seems to be nothing the least necessary in this, considering it just by itself. That no world should ever exist at all is perfectly comprehensible and seems to express not the slightest absurdity. Considering any particular item in the world it seems not at all necessary that the totality of these things, or any totality of things, should ever exist.

From the principle of sufficient reason it follows, of course, that there must be a reason not only for the existence of everything in the world but for the world itself, meaning by "the world" simply everything that ever does exist, except God, in case there is a god. This principle does not imply that there must be some purpose or goal for everything, or for the totality of all things; for explanations need not be, and in fact seldom are, teleological or purposeful. All the principle requires is that there be some sort of reason for everything. And it would certainly be odd to maintain that everything in the world owes its existence to something, that nothing in the world is either purely accidental, or such that it just bestows its own being upon itself, and then to deny this of the world itself. One can indeed *say* that the world is in some sense a pure accident, that there simply is no reason at all why this or any world should exist, and one can equally say that the world exists by its very nature, or is an inherently necessary being. But it is at least very odd and arbitrary to deny of this existing world the need for any sufficient reason, whether independent of itself or not, while presupposing that there is a reason for every other thing that ever exists.

Consider again the strange ball that we imagine has been found in the forest. Now, we can hardly doubt that there must be an explanation for the existence of such a thing, though we may have no notion what that explanation is. It is not, moreover, the fact of its having been found in the forest rather than elsewhere that renders an explanation necessary. It matters not in the least where it happens to be, for our question is not how it happens to be *there* but how it happens to be at all. If we in our imagination annihilate the forest, leaving only this ball in an open field, our conviction that it is a contingent thing and owes its existence to something other than itself is not reduced in the least. If we now imagine the field to be annihilated, and in fact everything else as well to vanish into nothingness, leaving only this ball to constitute the entire physical universe, then we cannot for a moment suppose that its existence has thereby been explained, or the need for any explanation eliminated, or that its existence is suddenly rendered self-explanatory. If we now carry this thought one step further and suppose that no other reality ever has existed or ever will exist, that this ball forever constitutes the entire physical universe, then we must still insist on there being some reason independent of itself why it should exist rather than not. If there must be a reason for the existence of any particular thing, then the necessity of such a reason is not eliminated by the mere supposition that certain other things do *not* exist. And again, it matters not at all what the thing in question is, whether it be large and complex, such as the world we actually find ourselves in, or whether it be something small, simple, and insignificant, such as a ball, a bacterium, or the merest grain of sand. We do not avoid the necessity of a reason for the existence of something merely by describing it in this way or that. And it would, in any event, seem quite plainly absurd to say that if the world were composed entirely of a single ball about six feet in diameter, or of a single grain of sand, then it would be contingent and there would have to be some explanation other than itself why such a thing exists, but that, since the actual world is vastly more complex than this, there is no need for an explanation of its existence, independent of itself.

BEGINNINGLESS EXISTENCE

It should now be noted that it is no answer to the question, why a thing exists, to state *how long* it has existed. A geologist does not suppose that she has explained why there should be rivers and mountains merely by pointing out that they are old. Similarly, if one were to ask, concerning the ball of which we have spoken, for some sufficient reason for its being, he would not receive any answer upon being told that it had been there since yesterday. Nor would it be any better answer to say that it had existed since before anyone could remember, or even that it had always existed; for the question was not one concerning its age but its existence. If, to be sure, one were to ask where a given thing came from, or how it came into being, then upon learning that it had always existed he would learn that it never really *came* into being at all; but he could still reasonably wonder why it should exist at all. If, accordingly, the world — that is, the totality of all things excepting God, in case there is a god — had really no beginning at all, but has always existed in some form or other, then there is clearly no answer to the question, where it came from and when; it did not, on this supposition, *come* from anything at all, at any time. But still, it can be asked why there is a world, why indeed there is a beginningless world, why there should have perhaps always been something rather than nothing. And, if the principle of sufficient reason is a good principle, there must be an answer to that question, an answer that is by no means supplied by giving the world an age, or even an infinite age.

CREATION

This brings out an important point with respect to the concept of creation that is often misunderstood, particularly by those whose thinking has been influenced by Christian ideas. People tend to think that creation — for example, the creation of the world by God — *means* creation *in time*, from which it of course logically follows that if the world had no beginning in time, then it cannot be the creation of God. This, however, is erroneous, for creation means essentially *dependence*, even in Christian theology. If one thing is the creation of another, then it depends for its existence on that other, and this is perfectly consistent with saying that both are eternal, that neither ever came into being, and hence, that neither was ever created at any point of time. Perhaps an analogy will help convey this point. Consider, then, a flame that is casting beams of light. Now, there seems to be a clear sense in which the beams of light are dependent for their existence upon the flame, which is their source, while the flame, on the other hand, is not similarly dependent for its existence upon them. The beams of light arise from the flame, but the flame does not arise from them. In this sense, they are the creation of the flame; they derive their existence from it. And none of this has any reference to time; the relationship of dependence in such a case would not be altered in the slightest if we supposed that the flame, and with it the beams of light, had always existed, that neither had ever *come* into being.

Now if the world is the creation of God, its relationship to God should be thought of in this fashion; namely, that the world depends for its existence upon God, and could not exist independently of God. If God is eternal, as those who believe in God generally assume, then the world may (though it need not) be eternal too, without that altering in the least its dependence upon God for its existence, and hence without altering its being the creation of God. The supposition of God's eternality, on the other hand, does not by itself imply that the world is eternal too; for there is not the least reason why something of finite duration might not depend for its existence upon something of infinite duration — though the reverse is, of course, impossible.

GOD

If we think of God as "the creator of heaven and earth," and if we consider heaven and earth to include everything that exists except God, then we appear to have, in the foregoing considerations, fairly strong reasons for asserting that God, as so conceived, exists. Now of course most people have much more in mind than this when they think of God, for religions have ascribed to God ever so many attributes that are not at all implied by describing him merely as the creator of the world; but that is not relevant here. Most religious persons do, in any case, think of God as being at least the creator, as that being upon which everything ultimately depends, no matter what else they may say about Him in addition. It is, in fact, the first item in the creeds of Christianity that God is the "creator of heaven and earth." And, it seems, there are good metaphysical reasons, as distinguished from the persuasions of faith, for thinking that such a creative being exists.

If, as seems clearly implied by the principle of sufficient reason, there must be a reason for the existence of heaven and earth — i.e., for the world — then that reason must be found either in the world itself, or outside it, in something that is literally supranatural, or outside heaven and earth. Now if we suppose that the world — i.e., the totality of all things except God — contains within itself the reason for its existence, we are supposing that it exists by its very nature, that is, that it is a necessary being. In that case there would, of course, be no reason for saying that it must depend upon God or anything else for its existence; for if it exists by its very nature, then it depends upon nothing but itself, much as the sun depends upon nothing but itself for its heat. This, however, is implausible, for we find nothing about the world or anything in it to suggest that it exists by its own nature, and we do find, on the contrary, ever so many things to suggest that it does not. For in the first place, anything that exists by its very nature must necessarily be eternal and indestructible. It would be a self-contradiction to say of anything that it exists by its own nature, or is a necessarily existing thing, and at the same time to say that it comes into being or passes away, or that it ever could come into being or pass away. Nothing about the world seems at all like this, for concerning anything in the world, we can perfectly easily think of it as being annihilated, or as never having existed in the first place, without there being the slightest hint of any absurdity in such a supposition. Some of the things in the universe are, to be sure, very old; the moon, for example, or the stars and the planets. It is even possible to imagine that they have always existed. Yet it seems quite impossible to suppose that they owe their existence to nothing but themselves, that they bestow existence upon themselves by their very natures, or that they are in themselves things of such nature that it would be impossible for them not to exist. Even if we suppose that something, such as the sun, for instance, has existed forever, and will never cease, still we cannot conclude just from this that it exists by its own nature. If, as is of course very doubtful, the sun has existed forever and will never cease, then it is possible that its heat and light have also existed forever and will never cease; but that would not show that the heat and light of the sun exist by their own natures. They are obviously contingent and depend on the sun for their existence, whether they are beginningless and everlasting or not.

There seems to be nothing in the world, then, concerning which it is at all plausible to suppose that it exists by its own nature, or contains within itself the reason for its existence. In fact, everything in the world appears to be quite plainly the opposite, namely, something that not only need not exist, but at some time or other, past or future or both, does not in fact exist. Everything in the world seems to have a finite duration, whether long or short. Most things, such as ourselves, exist only for a short while; they come into being, then soon cease. Other things, like the heavenly bodies, last longer, but they are still corruptible, and from all that we can gather about them, they too seem destined eventually to perish. We arrive at the conclusion, then, that although the world may contain some things that have always existed and are destined never to perish, it is nevertheless doubtful that it contains any such thing, and, in any case, everything in the world is capable of perishing, and nothing in it, however long it may already have existed and however long it may yet remain, exists by its own nature but depends instead upon something else.

Although this might be true of everything in the world, is it necessarily true of the world itself? That is, if we grant, as we seem forced to, that nothing in the world exists by its own nature, that everything in the world is contingent and perishable, must we also say that the world itself, or the totality of all these perishable things, is also contingent and perishable? Logically, we are not forced to, for it is logically possible that the totality of all perishable things might itself be imperishable, and hence, that the world might exist by its own nature, even though it is composed exclusively of things that are contingent. It is not logically necessary that a totality should share the defects of its members. For example, even though every person is mortal, it does not follow from this that the human race, or the totality of all people, is also mortal; for it is possible that there will always be human beings, even though there are no human beings who will always exist. Similarly, it is possible that the world is in itself a necessary thing, even though it is composed entirely of things that are contingent.

This is logically possible, but it is not plausible. For we find nothing whatever about the world, any more than in its parts, to suggest that it exists by its own nature. Concerning anything in the world, we have not the slightest difficulty in supposing that it should perish, or even that it should never have existed in the first place. We have almost as little difficulty in supposing this of the world itself. It might be somewhat hard to think of everything as utterly perishing and leaving no trace whatever of its ever having been, but there seems to be not the slightest difficulty in imagining that the world should never have existed in the first place. We can, for instance, perfectly easily suppose that nothing in the world had ever existed except, let us suppose, a single grain of sand, and we can thus suppose that this grain of sand has forever constituted the whole universe. Now if we consider just this grain of sand, it is quite impossible for us to suppose that it exists by its very nature and could never have failed to exist. It clearly depends for its existence upon something other than itself, if it depends on anything at all. The same will be true if we consider the world to consist not of one grain of sand but of two, or of a million, or, as we in fact find, of a vast number of stars and planets and all their minuter parts.

It would seem, then, that the world, in case it happens to exist at all — and this is quite beyond doubt — is contingent and thus dependent upon something other than itself for its existence, if it depends upon anything at all. And it must depend upon something, for otherwise there could be no reason why it exists in the first place. Now, that upon which the world depends must be something that either exists by its own nature or does not. If it does not exist by its own nature, then it, in turn, depends for its existence upon something else, and so on. Now then, we can say either of two things; namely, (1) that the world depends for its existence upon something else, which in turn depends on still another thing, this depending upon still another, *ad infinitum;* or (2) that the world derives its existence from something that exists by its own nature and that is accordingly eternal and imperishable, and is the creator of heaven and earth. The first of these alternatives, however, is impossible, for it does not render a sufficient reason why anything should exist in the first place. Instead of supplying a reason why any world should exist, it repeatedly begs off giving a reason. It explains what is dependent and perishable in terms of what is itself dependent and perishable, leaving us still without a reason why perishable things should exist at all, which is what we are seeking. Ultimately, then, it would seem that the world, or the totality of contingent or perishable things, in case it exists at all, must depend upon something that is necessary and imperishable, and that accordingly exists, not in dependence upon something else, but by its own nature.

"SELF-CAUSED"

What has been said thus far gives some intimation of what meaning should be attached to the concept of a self-caused being, a concept that is quite generally misunderstood, sometimes even by scholars. To say that something — God, for example — is self-caused, or is the cause of its own existence, does not mean that this being brings itself into existence, which is a perfectly absurd idea. Nothing can *bring* itself into existence. To say that something is self-caused *(causa sui)* means only that it exists, not contingently or in dependence upon something else but by its own nature, which is only to say that it is a being which is such that it can neither come into being nor perish. Now, whether in fact such a being exists or not, there is in any case no absurdity in the idea. We have found, in fact, that the principle of sufficient reason seems to point to the existence of such a being, as that upon which the world, with everything in it, must ultimately depend for its existence.

"NECESSARY BEING"

A being that depends for its existence upon nothing but itself and is in this sense self-caused, can equally be described as a necessary being; that is to say, a being that is not contingent, and hence not perishable. For in the case of anything that exists by its own nature and is dependent upon nothing else, it is impossible that it should not exist, which is equivalent to saying that it is necessary. Many persons have professed to find the gravest difficulties in this concept, too, but that is partly because it has been confused with other notions. If it makes sense to speak of anything as an *impossible* being, or something that by its very nature does not exist, then it is hard to see why the idea of a necessary being, or something that in its very nature exists, should not be just as comprehensible. And of course, we have not the slightest difficulty in speaking of something, such as a square circle or a formless body, as an impossible being. And if it makes sense to speak of something as being perishable, contingent, and dependent upon something other than itself for its existence, as it surely does, then there seems to be no difficulty in thinking of something as imperishable and dependent upon nothing other than itself for its existence.

"FIRST CAUSE"

From these considerations we can see also what is properly meant by a "first cause," an appellative that has often been applied to God by theologians and that many persons have deemed an absurdity. It is a common criticism of this notion to say that there need not be any first cause, because the series of causes and effects that constitute the history of the universe might be infinite or beginningless and must, in fact, be infinite in case the universe itself had no beginning in time. This criticism, however, reflects a total misconception of what is meant by a first cause. *First* here does not mean first in time, and when God is spoken of as a first cause He is not being described as a being that, at some time in the remote past, *started* everything. To describe God as a first cause is only to say that He is literally a *primary* rather than a secondary cause, an *ultimate* rather than a derived cause, or a being upon which all other things, heaven and earth, ultimately depend for their existence. It is, in short, only to say that God is the creator, in the sense of creation previously explained. Now this, of course, is perfectly consistent with saying that the world is eternal or beginningless. As we have seen, one gives no reason for the existence of a world merely by giving it an age, even if it is supposed to have an infinite age. To use a helpful analogy, we can say that the sun is the first cause of daylight and, for that matter, of the moonlight of the night as well, which means only that daylight and moonlight ultimately depend upon the sun for their existence. The moon, on the other hand, is only a secondary or derivative cause of its light. This light would be no less dependent upon the sun if we affirmed that it had no beginning, for an ageless and beginningless light requires a source no less than an ephemeral one. If we supposed that the sun has always existed, and with it its light, then we would have to say that the sun has always been the first — *i.e.*, the primary or ultimate — cause of its light. Such is precisely the manner in which God should be thought of, and is by theologians often thought of, as the first cause of heaven and earth.

THE NATURE OF THE WORLD

Thus far we have considered nothing about the world except the bare fact of its existence, an existence that, it has seemed, is contingent rather than necessary. It matters not, so far as concerns anything said so far, whether the world is orderly or chaotic, large or small, simple or complex, for the ideas so far elicited would still have whatever force they do have even if we supposed the world to consist of nothing more than the merest grain of sand.

Many persons, however, have thought that the nature or character of the world and its parts point most clearly to the existence of some supranatural "guiding hand," that is, to some *purposeful* being who, whether he created the world or not, nevertheless fashioned it. What is significant here is not merely that some world or other exists, but rather that it is the kind of world we find. What we find is not a mere grain of sand, nor a conglomeration of these or similar things, nor a chaos. We find an order and harmony, to say nothing of the mystery and complexity of things that our profoundest science and learning seem only barely to penetrate. Students are sometimes awed by the beautiful machinery and apparently purposeful design of the universe when they receive their initiation into science, whether this is discovered by them in the smallest parts of nature, particularly living things, or in the vastness of the heavens. Of course this orderliness is before our eyes all the time, but we hardly notice it, simply because we are so accustomed to it that we tend to take it for granted. The homeostasis or self-regulation of our own bodies, for instance, whereby the body manages to maintain the most unbelievable internal harmony and to adapt itself to the most diverse and subtle forces acting upon it, represents a wonder that human art cannot really duplicate and our science only dimly comprehends. Yet most people live out their lives without even noticing this seeming miracle that is perpetually before them. The same type of order and seemingly goal-directed change is apparent in the embryological development of living things.

This suggests another feature of the world that, in case it is real and not merely apparent, tends to cast doubt upon the supposition that the world we find ourselves in is the accidental and unintended result of the interacting forces of physical nature; namely, that some things in the world, particularly living organisms, seem purposeful or goal-directed in their very construction. Much modern biology is predicated on the supposition that such seemingly purposeful construction is only apparent and not real; indeed, the main significance of Darwin's work was that he made a convincing case for this. Yet, apart from the requirements of a more or less unconsciously held scientific orthodoxy, it is by no means obvious that this is so. If one considers any living thing whatever, he finds that its powers and construction are perfectly adapted to its mode of life. A hawk, for example, has sharp talons, rapacious beak, keen eyes, strength, and a digestive system all perfectly suited to a predatory mode of life. A lowly spider has likewise precisely what is needed in order to entrap its prey in artfully contrived snares. So it is with every creature whatever. Its anatomy, powers, and instincts are perfectly suited to its goal or mode of life. One can, of course, insist that it is only *because* such beings are so equipped that they pursue the goals they do, and deny that they are so equipped *in order to* pursue those goals, just as one can insist that it is only *because* a person is carrying rod and reel that he goes fishing, and deny that he is carrying this equipment *in order to* fish; but this seems artificial, even if one gives the evolutionary theory of the origin of such creatures everything that it claims.

The considerations barely adumbrated here fall into a whole cluster of arguments that are called, loosely, "the argument from design." The common element in them is that they all endeavor to establish the existence of some supranatural and creative being or beings from a consideration of the apparently artful and purposeful design manifested in the world, particularly in living things. We cannot go into a discussion of these arguments, for they are already embodied in an abundant literature and are for the most part inconclusive anyway. There is, however, one way of expressing the argument from design that has a peculiarly rational twist and that has, moreover, been hardly more than dimly perceived by most of those who have considered this subject. It rests upon the consideration that our own faculties of sense and cognition are not only remarkable in themselves but are in fact relied upon by us for the discovery of truth. It is this, and its implications, that we want now to consider.

CHANCE AND EVIDENCE

The idea we want to develop here is not easy to grasp without misunderstanding, so it will be best to approach it stepwise by considering first an example or two that should make it quite obvious.

Suppose that you are riding in a railway coach and glancing from the window at one of the stops; you see numerous white stones scattered about on a small hillside near the train in a pattern resembling these letters: THE BRITISH RAILWAYS WELCOMES YOU TO WALES. Now you could scarcely doubt that these stones do not just accidentally happen to exhibit that pattern. You would, in fact, feel quite certain that they were purposefully *arranged* that way to convey an intelligible message. At the same time, however, you could not prove, just from a consideration of their arrangement alone, that they were arranged by a purposeful being. It is possible — at least logically so — that there was no guiding hand at all in back of this pattern, that it is simply the result of the operations of inanimate nature. It is possible that the stones, one by one, rolled down the hill and, over the course of centuries, finally ended up in that interesting arrangement, or that they came in some other accidental way to be so related to one another. For surely the mere fact that something has an interesting or striking shape or pattern and thus *seems* purposefully arranged is no proof that it is. There might always be some other explanation. Snowflakes, viewed under magnification, exhibit symmetrical, interesting, and often beautiful shapes, and yet we know that these are not designed but can be explained simply in terms of the physics of crystallization. We find *apparently* purposeful arrangements and contrivances around us all the time, but we cannot always conclude that these are in fact the expressions of any purpose. Our own bodies and their organs seem purposeful not only in their individual structures but in their relationships to one another, and yet there are well-known theories, resting on such nonpurposeful concepts as chance variation, natural selection, and so on, that are able, at least in the opinion of many learned people, to explain these structures without introducing any ideas of purpose and design at all.

Here, however, is the important point it is easy to overlook; namely, that *if*, upon seeing from the train window a group of stones arranged as described, you were to conclude that you were entering Wales, and *if* your sole reason for thinking this, whether it was in fact good evidence or not, was that the stones were so arranged, *then* you could not, consistently with that, suppose that the arrangement of the stones was accidental. You would, in fact, be presupposing that they were arranged that way by an intelligent and purposeful being or beings for the purpose of conveying a certain message having nothing to do with the stones themselves. Another way of expressing the same point is that it would be *irrational* for you to regard the arrangement of the stones as evidence that you were entering Wales, and at the same time to suppose that they might have come to have that arrangement accidentally, that is, as the result of the ordinary interactions of natural or physical forces. If, for instance, they came to be so arranged over the course of time simply by their rolling down the hill, one by one, and finally just happening to end up that way, or if they were strewn upon the ground that way by the forces of an earthquake or storm or whatnot, then their arrangement would in no sense constitute evidence that you were entering Wales, or for anything whatever unconnected with themselves.

Consider another example. Suppose a stone were dug up and found to be covered with interesting marks, all more or less the same size and more or less in rows. Now there is nothing very remarkable about that. Glaciers and volcanoes have produced stones no less interesting in abundance. They may at first sight seem purposefully fabricated, but a geologist who knows how they came to be there can usually explain their interesting shapes and properties. Suppose further, however, that the marks on this stone are found to resemble the characters of an ancient alphabet. This, too, does not prove that they were purposefully inscribed, for natural forces can leave such marks as these on stones, and over the course of millions of years it is entirely possible that this should occasionally happen. There are places where one can, at will, pick up stones that are almost perfect rectangles and look exactly as though they were hewn by stonecutters, though in fact they resulted from glaciation. But now suppose that these marks are recognized by a scholar having a knowledge of that alphabet, and that with considerable uncertainty due to the obscurity of some of the marks and the obliteration of others, he renders a translation of them as follows: HERE KIMON FELL LEADING A BAND OF ATHENIANS AGAINST THE FORCES OF XERXES. Now one can, to be sure, still maintain that the marks are accidental, that they are only scratches left by volcanic activity, and that it is only a singular coincidence that they resemble, more or less, some intelligible message. Nature sometimes produces effects hardly less interesting and arresting than this. The point to make again, however, is this: If anyone having a knowledge of this stone concludes, solely on the basis of it, that there was someone named Kimon who died in battle near where this stone was found, then he cannot, rationally, suppose that the marks on the stone are the result of the chance or purposeless operations of the forces of nature. He must, on the contrary, assume that they were inscribed there by someone whose purpose was to record an historical fact. If the marks had a purposeless origin, as from volcanic activity or whatnot, then they cannot reveal any fact whatever except, perhaps, certain facts about themselves or their origin. It would, accordingly, be irrational for anyone to suppose *both* that what is seemingly expressed by the marks is true, and *also* that they appeared as the result of nonpurposeful forces, provided the marks are his *sole* evidence for believing that what they seem to say is true.

SENSATION AND EVIDENCE

Our own organs of sense, to say nothing of our brains and nervous systems, are things of the most amazing and bewildering complexity and delicacy. No matter how far and minutely psychologists and physiologists press their studies of these organs, they seem hardly any closer to a real understanding of them, and how they enable us to *perceive* the world around us. At best they discover only how they convey stimuli and impress physical changes upon the brain. Theories of perception, drawing upon all the scientific and physiological knowledge accumulated to date, are hardly less crude than the speculations of the Greeks.

Some of these organs, moreover, strikingly resemble things purposefully designed and fabricated by men, though they greatly exceed in their delicacy and versatility anything men have invented. The parts and structure of the eye, for example, closely resemble those of a camera. Yet the comparison of these, however striking, is superficial, for the eye does not take pictures. Unlike a camera, it somehow enables its possessor to perceive and thereby to understand. Things like this can be more or less imitated by men, but they are usually crude and makeshift in comparison. It is sometimes almost irresistible, when considering such a thing as the eye, to suppose that, however it may have originated, it is constructed in that manner *in order to* enable its possessor to see. Many persons quite naturally think in these terms, without at all realizing the implications of such purposeful or teleological conceptions.

It must be noted, however, that just as it is possible for a collection of stones to present a novel and interesting arrangement on the side of a hill, and for marks to appear on a stone in a manner closely resembling some human artifact, and for these things still to be the accidental result of natural, nonpurposeful forces, so also it is possible for such things as our own organs of sense to be the accidental and unintended results, over ages of time, of perfectly impersonal, nonpurposeful forces. In fact, ever so many biologists believe that this is precisely what has happened, that our organs of sense are in no real sense purposeful things, but only appear so because of our failure to consider how they might have arisen through the normal workings of nature. It is supposed, for example, that if we apply the conceptions of chance mutations and variations, natural selection, and so on, then we can see how it is at least possible — perhaps even almost inevitable — that things of this sort should finally emerge, without any purpose behind them at all.

It would be astonishing indeed if a quantity of stones were hurled into the air and fell to earth in a pattern spelling out some intelligible message. Anyone would feel, quite irresistibly, that it had been somehow *arranged* that they should fall that way. It would be less astonishing, however, if those stones were thrown a million times, and sooner or later fell to earth in such a pattern. Our astonishment would be still less if we found some perfectly natural, nonpurposeful explanation why they might sooner or later fall in that manner and, having so fallen, be thus preserved. If, for instance, we found that the stones were of slightly different weights, sizes, and shapes, that these influenced how they were thrown and how they rolled upon landing, that these slight differences tended to favor the likelihood that certain ones would come to rest in the striking manner in which they do come to rest, and that certain obstructions on the ground would tend to preserve them in this arrangement, and so on, then we might find it entirely plausible how they might fall as they do without the intervention of any purposeful being at all. If our explanation were of this kind, however, then, as noted before, their arrangement would constitute no evidence whatever for anything not causally connected with themselves.

The mere complexity, refinement, and seemingly purposeful arrangement of our sense organs do not, accordingly, constitute any conclusive reason for supposing that they are the outcome of any purposeful activity. A natural, nonpurposeful explanation of them is possible, and has been attempted — successfully, in the opinion of many.

The important point, however, and one that is rarely considered is that we do not simply *marvel* at these structures, and wonder how they came to be that way. We do not simply view them as amazing and striking things, and speculate upon their origins. We, in fact, whether justifiably or not, *rely* on them for the discovery of things that we suppose to be true and that we suppose to exist quite independently of those organs themselves. We suppose, without even thinking about it, that they reveal to us things that have nothing to do with themselves, their structures, or their origins. Just as we supposed that the stones on the hill told us that we were entering Wales — a fact having nothing to do with the stones themselves — so also we suppose that our senses in some manner "tell us" what is true, at least sometimes. The stones on the hill could, to be sure, have been an accident, in which case we cannot suppose that they really tell us anything at all. So also, our senses and all our faculties could be accidental in their origins, and in that case they do not really tell us anything either. But the fact remains that we do trust them, without the slightest reflection on the matter. Our seeing something is often thought to be, quite by itself, a good reason for believing that the thing exists, and it would be absurd to suggest that we *infer* this from the structure of our eyes as speculations upon their evolutionary origins. And so it is with our other faculties. Our remembering something is often considered to be, quite by itself, a good reason for believing that the thing remembered did happen. Our hearing a sound is often considered, quite by itself, a good reason for believing that a sound exists; and so on.

We are not here suggesting that our senses are infallible, nor even that we ought to rely upon their testimony. The point is that we do rely upon them. We do not believe merely that our senses are remarkably interesting things. We do not believe merely that they produce interesting effects within us, nor merely that they produce beliefs in us. We assume, rightly or wrongly, that they are *trustworthy* guides with respect to what is true, and what exists independently of our senses and their origins; and we still assume this, even when they are our only guides.

We saw that it would be irrational for anyone to say *both* that the marks he found on a stone had a natural, nonpurposeful origin and *also* that they reveal some truth with respect to something other than themselves, something that is not merely inferred from them. One cannot rationally believe both of these things. So also, it is now suggested, it would be irrational for one to say *both* that his sensory and cognitive faculties had a natural, nonpurposeful origin and *also* that they reveal some truth with respect to something other than themselves, something that is not merely inferred from them. If their origin can be entirely accounted for in terms of chance variations, natural selection, and so on, without supposing that they somehow embody and express the purposes of some creative being, then the most we can say of them is that they exist, that they are complex and wondrous in their construction, and are perhaps in other respects interesting and remarkable. We cannot say that they are, entirely by themselves, reliable guides to any truth whatever, save only what can be inferred from their own structure and arrangement. If, on the other hand, we do assume that they are guides to some truths having nothing to do with themselves, then it is difficult to see how we can, consistently with that supposition, believe them to have arisen by accident, or by the ordinary workings of purposeless forces, even over ages of time.

At this point persons who have a deep suspicion of all such arguments as this, and particularly persons who are hostile to any of the claims of religion, are likely to seize upon innumerable objections of a sort that it would hardly occur to anyone to apply to our first two examples, involving the stones. Thus, it is apt to be said that our cognitive faculties are not so reliable as some would suppose, which is irrelevant; or that arguments from analogy prove nothing, which is also irrelevant, because none of the foregoing is an argument from analogy. Or it is claimed that we rely on our cognitive faculties only because we have found them reliable in the past, and thus have a sound inductive basis for our trust, which is absurd, if not question-begging. The reason I believe there is a world around me is, quite simply, that I see it, feel it, hear it, and am in fact perpetually in cognitive contact with it, or at least assume myself to be, without even considering the matter. To suggest that I *infer* its existence from the effects that it has within me, and that I find the inference justified on the ground that such inner effects have, in the past, been accompanied by external causes, is not only a ridiculous caricature but begs the question of how, without relying upon my faculties, I could ever confirm such an idea in the first place. Again, it is sometimes said that the capacity to grasp truths has a decided value to the survival of an organism, and that our cognitive faculties have evolved, quite naturally, through the operation of this principle. This appears farfetched, however, even if for no other reason than that our capacity to understand what is true, through reliance upon our senses and cognitive faculties, far exceeds what is needed for survival. One might as well say that the sign on the hill welcoming tourists to Wales originated over the course of ages purely by accident, and has been preserved by the utility it was then found to possess. This is of course possible, but also immensely implausible.

THE SIGNIFICANCE OF THESE ARGUMENTS

It would be extravagant indeed to suppose that these reflections amount to any sort of confirmation of religion, or even that they have much to do with religion. They are purely metaphysical and philosophical considerations having implications of only a purely speculative kind. Even if they are utterly probative, which is of course controversial, it can still be pointed out, correctly, that they are consistent with ever so many views that are radically inconsistent with religion. They imply almost nothing with respect to any divine attributes, such as benevolence, and one could insist with some justification that even the word *God*, which is supposed to be the proper name of a personal being and not just a label to be attached to metaphysically inferred things, is out of place in them.

No more is claimed for these arguments, however, than that they are good arguments, and that they seem to yield the conclusion derived from them. If they are defective, the defects are not gross or obvious. The reader may suit himself whether they yield those conclusions, and if so, what their human significance might be.

CHAPTER TWELVE

Polarity

There is a common way of thinking that we can call *polarization*, and that appears to be the source of much metaphysics. It consists of dividing things into two exclusive categories, and then supposing that if something under consideration does not belong to one of them, then it must belong in the other. "Either/or" is the pattern of such thought, and because it is usually clear, rigorous, and incisive, it is also often regarded by philosophers as uniquely rational. Not surprisingly, it is presupposed in logic texts, in which we are told, on the first page, that every proposition is *either* true *or* false — and the abstract science of logic proceeds from there. Legal reasoning is also sometimes polarized, for the skill of an attorney or judge in defending a point of view is likely to rest upon his ability to lead his audience down the path he wants them to take by foreclosing, one after another, every bypath. "Guilty or innocent," "taxable or exempt," "lawful or unlawful," "sane or insane" are the kinds of choices he offers, with no opportunity to reject both or to accept a mixture.

Philosophers have cultivated polarized thought since the time of Socrates, who was the master of it. Thus Socrates characteristically gave his opponent a choice between two answers and, one of them being accepted, another choice immediately arose, giving rise to still another, until the opponent found himself face to face with some conclusion, usually a highly implausible one, that he could not back away from, every path of retreat having been closed off by the choices already made. And Socrates would then represent this strange conclusion as something not known before, which had been "learned" by this dialectical procedure.

Polarized thinking is not, however, the invention of philosophers. It is very common, almost natural, to anyone who thinks at all. For example, it is quite common for people to suppose that if a given action — killing one person to save another, for example — is not "wrong," then it must be "right," at least in the sense of being allowable. It is not considered possible that it might be both. Or again, it seems like common sense to say that a given person must be either married or unmarried — "You can't have it both ways"; or that someone either is in, say, Wisconsin, or he is not in Wisconsin — "You can't be two places at once"; or that at a given date and place it either rained, or it did not rain — and so on.

Of course, such thinking has great practical value. It is in fact required for the most common choices we make. People are often much bothered by the "morality" of their actions, for instance, and need some way to categorize them with respect to rightness or wrongness; hence the avid search for "ethical principles" that will somehow enable them to do this. Similarly, someone might be most eager to know whether some person of interest to him is "married" or not; much can depend on it. And it could be crucial to a prosecuting attorney whether someone he has charged with a crime was or was not in Wisconsin at a given time.

And, let it be said at once, things usually *can* be at least roughly categorized in these ways. For example, there usually is a definite answer, yes or no, to the question whether a given person is, say, in Wisconsin at a given moment. Note, however, that the crucial words in those two sentences are *usually* and *roughly*. The principle of polarity would have us use, instead, the words *always* and *exactly* in order to make our classifications sharp and precise. But, we are suggesting here, such sharpness and precision are sometimes bought at the expense of truth, for reality is far too loose a mixture of things to admit of such absolute distinctions. And sometimes, both in our practical affairs and in our philosophy, we are led into serious errors, which are fervently embraced just because they seem so clearly to have been proved.

THE EXCEPTIONABILITY OF POLARIZATIONS

Consider what would seem to be an obvious instance where the "either/or" pattern would fit without exception — for example, the statement that either it rained at a given place and time, or it did not. And let the place be Chicago, on some specific date — July 4, 1982, let us say. Now if it rained all over Chicago that day, then it assuredly rained then in Chicago. But what if it was a beautiful, fair day — except for a brief shower in some corner of that city. Did it rain in Chicago? The temptation is to say yes — for if there was any rain at all, then strictly speaking we have to say it rained. But suppose that on an exceptionally clear day a few raindrops fell in some remote corner of Chicago. Was the weather forecaster wrong who said the day before that it would be clear? Here we are tempted to say that, "strictly speaking," he was not quite right, but that practically speaking he was. But suppose there is but a single raindrop in my yard, along with others nearby. Did it rain in Chicago? Did it rain in my yard? In my entire yard? Or only part of it? Or only in this or that square inch of it? Or only at the spot where the drop fell? Or what?

One should resist the temptation to figure out (by drawing more distinctions) the "right" answers to these odd questions. There is no right answer. Either "yes" or "no" is as good an answer as the other. And the only thing odd about such questions is that there would seldom be any practical point in raising them. When questions of this sort arise in philosophy, however, then it does not matter whether there is any practical point in raising them, for philosophy does not pretend to be practical.

Consider the question whether, at a given moment, a certain person was or was not in Wisconsin. In most cases, of course, there will be a definite answer. But what of a passenger in an airplane flying over a corner of Wisconsin? Would he be lying if, some years later, he said he had never visited Wisconsin? Here the temptation is to say that, "strictly speaking," he would be mistaken, since we must include the space above Wisconsin within its geographical limits. But must we? How much space? Shall we say that astronauts, thousands of miles above earth, are nevertheless still passing through Wisconsin? And what does "above" mean here? How shall we determine what is "above" the earth and what "below" it? Surely we have here crossed over into nonsense. Nor will it help to go in the other direction, insisting that, "strictly speaking," one is in Wisconsin only if he is on the *terra firma* of that state — for in that case people would depart Wisconsin by the simple act of getting onto elevators. Nor should we split hairs by adding "or upon structures resting upon that *terra firma*," for someone who falls from a tree whose roots are planted in Wisconsin does not suddenly leave, and then as suddenly reenter, Wisconsin.

The point then is that with respect to such "either/or" choices, there are no right answers to be *found*; they can only be *invented*, and this is invariably done with an eye to practical consequences. But then you have to be careful not to view this invention, this "sharpening up" of a concept, as it is sometimes misleadingly described, as enabling you to express the truth more accurately than before. On the contrary, it distorts the truth by making reality appear to your mind to be more neat and tidy than it is.

PROBLEMS OF POPULAR METAPHYSICS

The danger just alluded to — that of producing "either/or" choices where "neither" or "both" would be a clearer approximation to truth, and of thus defining terms more precisely than the realities they are supposed to fit — sometimes produces inferences and "conclusions" that can have far-reaching effects. The danger is made more insidious by the illusion that one has "shown" something to be true that is not really true at all, often in areas where there simply is no actual truth to be shown.

For example, you sometimes find people, even educated people, trying to discern the borderline between life and death. Is someone whose heart and pulse are strong and normal, but whose brain has irreversibly ceased to function, still alive? What is the seat of life: the heart? or the brain? Questions like these, following the "either/or" pattern, invite answers, and there is an almost irresistible temptation to try to find them. Philosophy teachers sometimes engage their students in discussions of this kind, because they are invariably lively ones that "get the students thinking." It is seldom made clear that such thinking is in the nature of the case certain to end in failure. Sometimes, however, metaphysical wisdom begins not with finding an answer to a metaphysical question but with the realization that no answer exists, even, sometimes, to a question that is perfectly clear and precise.

Of course, answers to such questions can always be invented, and indeed they always are. But as with all inventions, they differ according to the predilections, needs, and prejudices of their inventors. In the realm of metaphysics the competing inventors of answers then fall to wrangling over which answer is the "true" one, quite failing to realize that no one has discovered any truth at all. The answers are in fact nothing but rival fabrications.

Here man is, indeed, the measure of things, in precisely the sense Protagoras meant. Rival answers to questions of this nature can all be declared to be true, which is but another way of saying that none is objectively true. But as Protagoras insisted, some answers are nevertheless *better* than others; better, that is, in terms of their consequences. So the answer one produces to such a question as that concerning the beginning or ending of life is going to be a function of what he wants to get out of that answer; or in other words, what its consequences will be. Declaring that a person's life ends when his heart finally stops will have decidedly different consequences from saying that it ends with the cessation of brain function. In the latter case, for instance, but not in the former, you can remove someone's healthy, pulsating heart, for whatever purpose — *e.g.*, to give it to someone else who needs it. You choose between answers by first deciding, consciously or otherwise, which consequences you like better. And there can be nothing wrong with this, for their simply is no other basis for choice.

Thus if you think about it, you can see that the correct answer in such cases as this does not fit the "either/or" pattern at all, but rather a pattern we can express as "some of each." For example, a person whose brain is forever dead but whose heart and other vital processes are normal is not quite dead, but neither is he quite alive; he is, *strictly speaking,* partly each. And here you have to resist the impulse to say, "But how can he be both dead and alive?" for that is only to betray a mindless dedication to the "either/or" thought pattern. It does not promote rigorous and precise thinking, but the very opposite. Nor should one be tempted to say that if anyone is partly still alive, then he is, after all, still living, and therefore, alive; for from the point of view of logic, it would be exactly as good to say that, if someone is partly dead — for instance, if his brain is dead, or any other part of him, such as a foot or a finger or indeed a hair on his head, then he is, after all, already *dead* — which is of course absurd. It is, moreover, well known that many of the body's cells are still living quite some time after death, by every traditional criterion, has set in; but no one is going to insist that someone is still "alive" just because a few cells in the hair follicles or fingernails are still multiplying.

The point then is that the transition from life to death, like most natural transitions, is a gradual one, and that no *borderline* between the two exists. Borderlines can be invented, of course, but they cannot be found, for they are not there.

COMING INTO BEING

The same will be true, of course, with respect to coming into existence. We tend to assume that any given thing either exists, or it does not, and that there can thus be no gradual transition into that state; but that is only because we long ago became the victims of polarized thought. Thus each of us is apt to suppose that, since he now exists, but at some past time (*e.g.*, one hundred years ago) did not, then there must have been some moment between then and now when he came into existence. Traditionally that time has been fixed as the moment of birth, but the relative arbitrariness of this is apparent to everyone. There is, for example, no *moment* of birth; birth is itself a process that takes time. But more important, existence obviously precedes birth which is nothing more than the passage, not into existence, but into the light of day.

Having noted this, one is then invited to work back to some imagined "moment" at which existence itself began. But existence of *what*? An ovum? a zygote? bonded genetic material? fused nuclei? life? a blastula? an embryo? a person? what?

And the next thing to note is, whichever of these one selects, *its* coming into existence is also a process, and not something that is achieved in a "moment." The beginnings of a particular ovum, for example, are nebulous and in no sense located at a point in time. The same is true of the formation of a human zygote, the various stages of which involve numerous complex and time-consuming processes on the parts of both male and female gametes, even after these have become more or less united and before their nuclei have become fused. This fusion of parent nuclei is in turn an unbelievably complex process that takes place over time, without discernible time of commencement or completion, nor is the genetic material of these nuclei bonded in a single instantaneous, or even very brief, time. The same can be said about the origins of the blastula, embryo, or any other stage of development that has received a biological name. The initial division of the fertilized ovum, which can perhaps be considered some sort of beginning of an organism, takes thirty-six hours, and not for another twenty-eight hours are there as many as four cells. And as for personhood, or life, these words obviously denote no *things* at all. Being a person is a quality with which some things, namely human beings, are invested, according to conventional criteria. So the question whether, for example, a tadpole, or a horse, or a zygote, "has" that quality is nothing more than the question whether we have found it useful, for legal or other purposes, to regard it that way. We have found no reason to treat tadpoles or horses as persons. Perhaps if one of them began using language intelligibly, or exhibited a potential to do so, then we would; perhaps we would not. Nor have human spermatozoans ever been treated as persons, nor human ova. Perhaps they are too numerous, or too small, but more likely, there would just be no point in so regarding them. The human zygote, however, in spite of its minuteness, *is* called a "person" by some, usually for theological reasons, though most people consider this absurd. Whether it is "really" a person or not is, of course, a metaphysical question, and one that has no answer, being a perfect expression of polarized thinking in an area where such thinking is certain to produce nonsense. For anyone to declare an undifferentiated human zygote to be a "person" is thus only to express a preference or choice, often one that has been guided by moral or religious presuppositions. It cannot, in the nature of the case, be a declaration of fact.

Still, one wants to say, I exist, and there was a time past when I did not. I must, therefore, whether instantly or otherwise, at some time have come into existence, and the solicitation seems overwhelming to find that time. Nor is it just a matter of metaphysical curiosity. Questions of religion and morality do seem to turn upon it. Even politicians find themselves drawn into the question of when "life" begins, and indeed, feelings on this strange question can be so intense as to ruin political careers.

What people actually seek in the pursuit of such questions is some dramatic or at least recognizable *event* in one's history that can be regarded as "the beginning" of life, or personhood, or humanity, or whatever. The trouble is, of course, that one's history is filled with more or less dramatic events that seem to mark beginnings of some sort, yet no such event seems to serve any better than some other as the beginning of life.

Thus, my awakening this morning was a beginning, more or less dramatic — but not the beginning of *me*, since I remember yesterday, and many days before that. So likewise was my birth a beginning, a fairly dramatic one, but for reasons already considered, it was not the beginning of *me* (except for certain purposes of law and custom, such as assigning me an age). *I* was there, in the womb, waiting to be born, before this happened. Of course, having pushed back to this point, virtually everyone then pushes back still farther, to some minute and unwitnessed event, vaguely described in such expressions as "the moment of conception," and there are persons who will solemnly declare, as if enunciating some kind of fact, even as a fact of biology, that this is an absolute beginning. But it obviously is not, for there is, again, no such "moment" — conception is a profoundly complex process that takes time — and furthermore, the elements that enter into that process were already living prior to then. From the standpoint of metaphysics, the "moment" of conception is no better choice for marking the passage into existence than the "moment" of birth. It only is earlier, less familiar, and hence more mysterious and more obscure.

Of course, one can simply abandon consideration of fact altogether, which is what usually happens with questions like this, and say, for example, quite arbitrarily, that God infuses a soul into a human ovum at some moment — usually, again, the "moment" of conception, converting it to a "person." But there is obviously no way of checking this, nor indeed, even knowing what one would be checking for. What kind of observation would count as either confirming or disconfirming it? What, indeed, does such a declaration even mean? It clearly arises, not from anything anyone knows or even believes, but simply from theological presupposition, or more often, from purely moral presuppositions. And in this case, of course, it is the theology or morality that is determining what is to be regarded as "fact," and not facts that are producing theological or moral inferences. Thus persons who, for whatever reason, happen to have an aversion to abortion are very likely to prefer one kind of description, whereas those who have no such aversion will prefer another, then the two sides will argue as *if* they were disputing certain facts — indeed, certain facts of biology — whereas they are only expressing their divergent and sometimes strong feelings about rival policies. And metaphysics, which is here invoked to resolve such a dispute, can obviously do nothing — except, of course, exacerbate it, by falsely appearing to provide a metaphysical foundation in support of one set of feelings or the other.

There are other familiar transitions of a more or less meaningful kind in which no one is ever tempted to seek out the "moment" of such transition, because no religious or moral feelings require it. When does a child become an adolescent? or an adolescent an adult? And on what day does one pass into middle age"? It is easy to see that, in spite of the fact that such transitions occur, there is no real time at which they begin or end. Often, when human needs require it, we *invent* such times. For example, an adolescent is declared suddenly to turn to an adult on his twenty-first birthday, sometimes his eighteenth. But everyone recognizes this as conventional. We *need* a date, for legal purposes. So we *declare* one, and we give it the force of law. But we do not find one. The same is quite obviously true with respect to the question: When did I become a person? Metaphysically, the answer to this is: I am a person; once I was not; hence I became a person — but there is no *time* at which this was accomplished. It occurred gradually, over a considerable time, and had no real beginning or ending. And the same line of thinking applies to such questions as: When did I begin to exist? When did I become human? and so on.

Of course, we would like our truths to be sharper, more incisive, more exact than that. But metaphysically, one has to see that, sharp or not, that is the *exact* truth, and anything more sharp and definite is *not* going to be exact.

POLARITY AND TRADITIONAL METAPHYSICS

Of course that is just one of the innumerable ways one can get bogged down philosophically by polarized thinking. The history of philosophy abounds with such illustrations. Indeed, it is probably no exaggeration to say that metaphysics has, from the beginning of philosophy, drawn more nourishment from this unfortunate source than from the mysterious and perplexing world itself.

Very early in the history of western philosophy, for example, Parmenides was driven to the outrageous metaphysical conclusion that there is no such thing as becoming or passing away, and hence, no change anywhere. What appears to us as motion and change must be simply illusion. Behind this incredible proposition lay a perfect example of polarization; namely, his supposition that, if something were to change, then something that *is* would cease to be, or in other words, become what is *not*, and that what is *not* would perforce come to *be*. His conclusion seemed to him inevitable, just because he allowed himself no choice of answers besides those offered within this "either/or" framework. His disciple Zeno, of Elea, arrived at similar conclusions by adhering to the same "rigorous" pattern of thought. Thus, for example, Zeno argued that anything that exists, in case it consists of parts, must be infinitely large, because (and here is the polarization) each such part either has some size, or it does not. But if each such part has size, then so also does each part of *it* — for example, each of its two halves; and each part of these, in turn, has size too, and so on, *ad infinitum*. You can never conceive of a part so small as to be without size, and hence without parts. Therefore, anything composed of parts is composed of infinitely many of them, each having some size, so the thing in question will be infinitely large. The only alternative to this (so Zeno thought) would be for it to have no size at all, and hence to be utterly nonexistent, this result following from the supposition that its "parts" have no size. Everything is therefore either infinitely large or infinitely small, filling the whole of space or none of it, or in other words, being identical with everything, or with nothing. Strange as this conclusion is, it can be quite rigorously deduced from the premises Zeno began with, together with his restriction of answers to just two possibilities.

Nor do metaphysicians seem to have learned of the pitfalls of polarized thinking with the passage of the centuries. It is quite common to find them, even now, earnestly engaged in disputation over issues having no other source. How much of the issue of fatalism, for example, rests upon the supposition that every declarative assertion must be either true or false? How often is it considered possible that some such assertions might be a bit of both, or perhaps neither? Why is it thought that the world must fit so exactly our neat and precise descriptions? Similarly, how much of the celebrated problem of free will turns on the supposition that everything that happens either is, or is not, causally determined? Why are these two choices thought to exhaust the possibilities?

BEING AND NON-BEING
AS EXCLUSIVE CATEGORIES

Still another area of metaphysics, and a very large one, that appears particularly susceptible to polarized thought is that which deals with questions of existence. Anything whatever, it would seem, either exists, or it does not — there can be no middle ground between these possibilities. Thus, the moon exists, as does the city of Paris, the Statue of Liberty, and the one hundred and first person appointed to the U.S. Supreme Court. The satellite of our moon, on the other hand, does not exist at all, nor does any unicorn, nor any daughter of the one hundred and first Supreme Court Justice, since all her children are male. Nor, it would seem, would it make sense to speak of any of these things as *partially* existing, or as belonging to some existential realm between being and nonbeing. The moon, for instance, cannot partially exist and partially not. Existence is something it simply has, and something its satellite lacks.

There are, to be sure, some things that have a dubious kind of existence, if any at all — numbers, for example, or abstract things such as justice, or fictional beings such as Hamlet, or entities such as the average taxpayer. These things have properties, about which one can discourse intelligibly, but metaphysicians can dispute whether they really exist.

That, however, does not concern us here, for we can simply limit ourselves to physical objects, to things that, in case they are real, can be located in space and seen — things like the Statue of Liberty, for instance. And concerning any of these, at least, we seem safe in saying that it either does exist, or it does not. No such thing has a merely partial existence.

Yet in spite of the seeming obviousness of this, and what would seem to be the unquestionable applicability of polarity here, it does have a consequence that is certainly *not* obvious and that seems, in fact, quite absurd; namely, that every existing object which at any time in history did not exist has sprung suddenly into existence at some moment of time. This seems to follow from the supposition that it at one time did not exist, then at a later time did, and that there can be no gradual transition from the one state to the other, during which it only partially exists.

This certainly does not seem in any sense true of such things as we have been considering. The Statue of Liberty, for instance, did not at some instant come into being all at once; yet it does exist, and there was a time when it did not.

Then what shall we say? The truth seems to be expressed best this way: that there was a time past when there was no Statue of Liberty at all; that there was a subsequent time, *e.g.*, yesterday, when it entirely existed; and that between those two times there was a considerable interval of time during which it was in the process of coming into existence; and further, that throughout that interval, it partially existed, and partially did not.

Now if that description is correct — and it does seem to be exactly correct — then polarity, as applied to questions of existence, is *not* correct. For existence appears to admit of degrees, like everything else.

Of course the temptation here is to break the thing in question down into parts and to say that the existence of each of these, at least, does not admit of degrees. But this, too, is apparently false. The head of that statue, for instance, came into existence quite gradually, as did the statue itself. And so with any other part. Of course its most minute parts — the atoms, perhaps, of which it is composed, in case there are such things — may *always* have existed, but that is not relevant. We are here dealing only with things that at one time did not exist, and we are saying that their existence is something they can acquire quite gradually, in spite of what our habits of polarized thinking may incline us to regard as obvious.

THE PROBLEM OF PERSONAL
IDENTITY OVER TIME

There is one metaphysical problem that seems to have resulted almost entirely from polarization, and that is the celebrated problem of personal identity. A part of that problem can be expressed in the following way: Am I the same person as that infant upon whom my mother bestowed my name? Or have I perhaps become someone else? This latter suggestion, the way it is put, seems so plainly dubious that philosophers are inclined to treat the alternative — that I am still the very same person — as axiomatic.

Generalizing the question, we may note that everyone, over the course of his life, undergoes great changes, some of them so radical that he seems finally to have lost his identity with his earlier self. He passes from infancy to old age, the two stages bearing almost no similarity to each other. In the course of this his body sometimes undergoes total renewal, such that none of the cells of the infant body are still possessed by that adult who, nevertheless, still considers himself as being in some sense "the same person" as the infant of years ago. The teeth, it is said, do not undergo such renewal, so that some of these, or parts of them, might in the strictest sense remain the same throughout one's lifetime. But of course, one sometimes loses all one's teeth, and has them replaced with false ones, so that even this continuity is destroyed.

Suppose, then, I pick out a certain child of several decades ago and say of him, "That is I," meaning that the child alluded to (me, as an infant) and the person alluding to him (me again, now as an adult) are one and the same person. I might pick out the child by a snapshot, for example ("That's me, on my mother's lap"), or by a document ("Here's my birth certificate — the person it says was born at that time and place to those parents is me,"), or in numerous other ways.

Now clearly, this identification does seem in some sense sometimes correct. There is some sense in which I am one and the same person as *one* of the infants shown in an old photograph, sitting on my mother's knee, and not at all the same as the other infant on the other knee, that being my twin brother. And yet, my body may have not a single cell or molecule in common with *either* of those infants. So in what sense am I nevertheless the same person as one of them, and not the same as the other?

It cannot be, of course, that I have the same properties, for I do not, or, to the slight extent that I do, then I share those same properties with the infant on the other knee, my brother. I have the property of being male, for instance, and so do both of those infants. I have the property of having a certain person as my mother — but again, so do both of those infants. And many, indeed virtually all, of my present properties are shared by *neither* of those infants — I am bearded, for example, and weigh more than one hundred pounds, and so on, unlike either of those infants, to *one* of which I nevertheless claim to be identical, and from the other of which I claim to be a totally different person.

What connects me with the one and not the other?

The answer is contained in the statement that I am *the same person* as the one but not the other. But what does that mean?

Metaphysicians, or at least a great many of them, have supposed it to mean that there is a strict identity in something, namely, a person, over the course of time. But since no such identity holds with respect to his body over the course of time — for the body is constantly being changed and renewed, no particle of it remaining indefinitely — then the person who is possessed of such identity must be something *other* than the physical or biological body. I am one thing, it is thought, that remains *the same* thing through time, and my body is something else, which becomes something quite different over the course of time, becoming, eventually, entirely or totally different from the body I once identified as "mine."

And this reflection, of course, at once gives rise to a great number of theories as to just what that person — a being *within* a body, as it would seem — actually is. Some imagine it to be the mind or soul. And it has even been seriously maintained that this *person*, which retains its strict identity through time, is nothing other than some invisibly minute particle of matter located, presumably, somewhere in the brain.

But clearly such bizarre theories, which provide endless delight to metaphysicians and their students, do not arise from any observations of people.

No one has ever *seen* a person, on such metaphysical accounts as these; we see only the everchanging bodies in which their persons are housed. This is, of course, why such theories are considered metaphysical in the first place. They arise from metaphysical reflection and in no way lend themselves either to confirmation or refutation by any actual observations.

But what *is* the character of the thought that produces such metaphysics? It is, plainly, polarized thought. It is assumed that a person either is one and the same as his former self, or else totally different, and since he cannot be totally different, we have to say he is one and the same.

But we do not have to think that way. Instead we can say that a person undergoes constant change and renewal over the course of time, such that he is in some respects the same today as he was yesterday and in some respects different, that over the course of sufficient time he undergoes a total renewal such that he shares no cell or particle with a former self long since past, but that he is nevertheless *the same person* in this relative sense, that he *grew out of* that former person. This is exactly the sense in which a butterfly, for example, is the same insect as the caterpillar from which it evolved, or the oak tree is the same plant as the tiny shoot that emerged from a certain acorn. The sameness is relative, but it is entirely sufficient for every claim we need to make about the identity of persons over time, whether the claims be moral, legal, or whatever. Thus: I am the same as *one* of the infants pictured sitting on my mother's knee in a very old photograph, but a different person from the other infant shown there, who is my twin brother. This means that, while no part or particle of my body is shared with either infant, and while I share as many common properties with the one as with the other, there is nevertheless a relationship that I have to one, and not to the other, quite well expressed by my saying that I grew out of the infant on the left knee, not the one on the right.

IDENTITY OVER TIME AND SPACE

Perhaps the easiest way to understand the identity of a person over a length of time is to compare it with the identity of a rope over a length of space.

Thus, think of a rope of considerable length, composed of individual fibers, none of which is as long as the rope itself. No fiber, accordingly, reaches from one end of the rope to the other. We can even suppose that the longest fiber in the rope is but a small fraction of the length of the rope. Hence the successive segments of the rope will consist of fibers, some of which extend into adjoining segments, overlapping fibers there, and some of which do not, and all of the fibers at either end of the rope will be different from those at the other end. Still, it is all one rope. If each of us pulls on a different end of it in a tug of war, we are assuredly pulling on the same rope. There is no need at all to assume some single fiber to continue unbroken through the length of the rope in order to ensure this identity. And we can say that each segment is continuous with or "emerges from" every anterior segment in a way similar to that in which a person is continuous with or "grows out of" every earlier chronological segment of his past. And to make the analogy complete, we can suppose that the length of rope we are considering arose in the following way: that from two previously existing ropes two fibers broke away and became entwined with each other to form a minute strand, then more strands became added to this, making it longer and larger until it grew into a complete length of rope in its own right. This illustrates the manner in which a rope might arise from two parent ropes and yet be an individual rope distinct from them and, by perfect analogy, the way in which a person derives his existence from his parents, and yet acquires an individual identity of his own, distinct from theirs, that persists through time.

ANOTHER IDENTITY PROBLEM

Metaphysicians sometimes concoct puzzles of identity, putting into them the very ingredients that seem to preclude solution. For example, it is well known that some human parts, tissues, and organs can be exchanged between people. It is not hard to transplant a hair from one person to another, for instance, and blood from one person can be transfused to another with relative ease. Kidneys, likewise, are sometimes transferred, and more recently, hearts and lungs. Suppose, then, that as a result of greatly improved techniques of neurosurgery, the brains of two persons — Mr. Brown and Mr. Robinson, let us call them — get exchanged, Brown ending up with Robinson's brain, and vice versa. Now further suppose that, after recovery from this rather radical surgical procedure, Brown — or the man who *looks* like Brown — goes home to Robinson's house and family, remembers all the things Robinson remembered, recognizes the people there as his wife and children, goes to Robinson's office and resumes the rather demanding and specialized work that Robinson had always done there so well, and so on. And make the same sort of assumptions about Robinson — that he (or what everyone supposes is he) emerges from the surgery with all of Brown's memories and associations, thinks that Brown's wife and children are his family, and so on.

Which one is really Brown, and which is really Robinson?

The trouble with this question is the way it is put, for it offers only two choices. Either this person who looks like Robinson but acts like Brown is Robinson, or he is Brown. And similarly for that person, who looks like Brown but acts like Robinson. It is simply assumed that the answer will have to be *one or the other*.

But there is no reason for us to accept this polarized and exclusive "either/or" presupposition. The "problem" simply disappears as a problem when we say that each of the persons emerging from this procedure is part Robinson, part Brown; and that neither is, strictly speaking, either Brown *or* Robinson.

The identity of either person over time has simply been abruptly destroyed by so radical a change as this, and we can no longer really say, of the persons we end up with, which grew out of Robinson, which out of Brown. Either claim would be as good as the other.

What we would have in such a case would not differ, metaphysically, from what we would have in the case of two cars whose parts were interchanged. If the tires of one are put on the other, we do not hesitate to say that it is still the same car, just as, in the case of a person, we think of him as preserving his identity even if he receives someone else's kidney, or even his heart. But if we purchased a car and then went back to the dealer to get it, only to learn that its engine had been replaced with another, we could certainly raise the question whether it was the same car. And if two cars, a Ford and a Plymouth, had their engines exchanged, and we then raised the question, which is the Ford, and which is the Plymouth, surely the correct answer would be: neither. Each car is part Ford, part Plymouth.

And in just exactly that way we should say, of our two men whose brains get swapped, that each is part Brown, part Robinson, this being the *whole* answer to the question. And if anyone were to press on and ask, but who is *really* Brown there, and who is really Robinson? Then he would *not* be expressing clear and precise metaphysical thinking at all. He would be displaying polarized thinking and exhibiting not a deeper sense of the problem but rather a failure to grasp it at all.

POLARIZATION AND COMMON SENSE

Metaphysical bewilderment sometimes results from our seeing clearly enough how things are but being unable to describe what we see. Thus everyone understands his relationship to that particular infant from which he developed, as well as he understands his relationship to his own mother. The problem lies simply in describing that relationship. Similarly, we easily see the result of exchanging, in imagination, two persons' brains as easily as we see the result of exchanging the engines of two cars. It is only a matter of describing what has happened, and the result. And the reason it is a problem is that we apply an "either/or" pattern, which works in most cases, to cases where that pattern does not fit. The result is metaphysics — not the kind of metaphysics that is a part of philosophical wisdom — but rather, the metaphysics of disputation, hair-splitting, and paradox, so dearly loved by some. The solutions to non-problems can only be non-solutions, however; and as these non-problems are sometimes the creations of our own thinking, the way through them is not through more of the same kind of thinking but rather through a revision of thought patterns themselves.

CHAPTER THIRTEEN

Metaphysics and Meaning

There are two basic impulses to study metaphysics. One, emphasized by Aristotle, is the need to understand *how* things come about and *how* they are connected to each other. The other is the need to know *why*, to understand the meaning of things and, especially, the meaning of one's own existence.

Thus a philosophical person cannot help asking: "Why am I here?" "What is the point of my existence?" "What is the meaning of my life?" "Indeed, has it any meaning? Or am I, like the lifeless and worthless things at my feet, just one more thing that exists, to no purpose?"

Of course shallow answers come readily to the minds of persons who are more clever than wise. They say that I am here because I was born, then offer an account of the process of conception and gestation — things already familiar. Or they say the question makes no sense, since meaning is a concept of language, not metaphysics. Words have meaning, they say, but a person does not.

But even if we suppose such observations to be true, and even incontestable, they do not satisfy the sense of wonder that characterizes a philosophical mind. There has got to be some possible point or significance to my life, something commensurate with the extraordinary fact of my existence that can give it meaning, something that can be won, but can also be missed.

To get hold of the question at a metaphysical level, then, I must first note that I share existence with every stick and stone, and that I share life itself with houseflies and snails; yet my being must have a meaning not shared by these. It would not matter if the stones at my feet or the housefly on the door screen had never existed at all.

Perhaps it would not matter had I never existed either. Ten minutes before my conception there was only one chance in several million that I would ever exist at all. Countless millions of actual persons, like myself, have come and gone before me, and virtually all were at once forgotten. Concerning any of these now nameless and forgotten souls, it would not matter had they never been. And so it is, no doubt, with me. Even in the unlikely event that I should win fame or glory, or even, perhaps, alter the very course of history by some extraordinary deeds, still, the very civilization of which I am a part, with its history, will someday belong to an all but forgotten past. Such has been the fate of great civilizations of the remote past, whose names are now known only to a few. And, in any case, few of us ever leave any mark on the world beyond the circle of family and friends who are, like ourselves, soon forgotten too.

RELIGION AND MEANING

Conventional religions, of course, supply an answer to the question of life's meaning. Our role, the religions of the world declare, is to serve God and humankind, and they declare that we will, in some sense, be judged according to how well we do this.

Now there is no doubt that persons persuaded of the truth and importance of religion find every reassurance there, and are not troubled by doubts concerning life's meaning. This is why Schopenhauer declared religion to be the metaphysics of the vulgar. Religion answers our deep need to understand the why of things and, especially, the meaning of our own lives. But its answers are drawn from faith or, which has come to mean the same thing, from tradition, rather than from one's own reason and observation. From the point of view of metaphysics, then, those answers are concocted from thin air. The fact that some declaration is comforting, that it is widely believed, and has been held to be true by our forefathers and by theirs, explains why it appeals to unphilosophical persons, but is no reason at all for supposing it to be true. And it is part of the task of metaphysics to teach us to *resist* what is merely comforting, and to rest our profoundest convictions on what has been thought out, what has been seen to be true by one's own unfettered mind, and not merely on what one has been taught. The religion that was imparted to you, perhaps as a child, may be precious to you, and it is not the responsibility of metaphysics to rob you of it. But it is, after all, religion, which is intellectually groundless, and not metaphysics, which, however difficult and elusive, is at least not utterly groundless.

To get hold of our question, then, let us consider our lives, not in the context of some prefabricated religious view, however venerable, but in the context of the actual world we live in, see, and know.

MEANINGLESS LIFE

Both our religious and political traditions have taught us to think of every human life as having an inherent worth. Human beings are thus thought of as unique within the whole of creation. But this is not the verdict of experience. Most of the people you see on the streets, coming and going, appear to live to no purpose beyond the present moment. The days come and go, each much like all the others, and through the minds of most persons pass only the most trivial thoughts, the concerns of the moment, a trifling victory here, a similarly insignificant defeat there, a succession of momentary pleasures, interrupted by insignificant frustrations. Even those whose lives are not a mindless going through motions usually have no greater purpose than some personal gratification, such as the accumulation of wealth, or power, or toys on a grand scale, or status — things that are no sooner won than new desires emerge as worthless as those already achieved. The great majority of humankind then pass from the stage and enter the oblivion of the millions, now forgotten, who have preceded them and whose lives were essentially no different.

Thus meaningful life is no birthright. It is something which, if it is to be had at all, must be won and, apparently, won against considerable odds. Most persons never achieve it at all.

MEANING AND TIME

Nothing, including human existence, gains meaning merely through the passage of time. That a human life should be prolonged adds nothing to its significance, in spite of the almost universal prejudice to the contrary. If it lacked meaning to begin with, then its prolongation is but an enlargement of that meaninglessness.

Time does, nonetheless, provide the *condition* for life's meaning, for it is the necessary condition for both personal and social history. History does not consist merely of a succession of events. If it were otherwise, then a clock, which did nothing but tick off the moments and the hours, could be said to have a history; or similarly, the surface of the sea, with its succession of turbulence and calm. That there is such a thing as human history is the result not merely of the fact that the generations perpetually arise and pass away, but rather, of the fact that human beings — or rather, some human beings — have a capacity to *create* things. And it is, as we shall see, this capacity to create, which we alone share with the gods, that gives our lives whatever meaning they have.

TIME IN A LIFELESS WORLD

To see this, let us begin by thinking of the whole of inanimate reality, that is, the entire world, as devoid of life. This would be a world without history or meaning. What happens in that world has happened before and, considering any event by itself, it makes no difference when it happens, nor even any sense to assign it a date. Time is here irrelevant. The earth turns, for example, but it makes not the least difference whether a given rotation is the millionth, or hundred millionth. Each turning is the same as the others, and no assigning of a number to this one or that has any significance. And so it is with everything else that happens in that lifeless world. A mountain rises gradually and is gradually eroded, but it makes no difference when this happens. And raindrops fall, but that a given raindrop should fall at one time rather than at another does not matter, nor is it even easy to make such temporal distinctions. Each drop is just like any other, and no newness is introduced by supposing that it falls earlier, or later, or even millions of years earlier or later. Combinations of events might occur which occur at no other time, to be sure, but they are already contained in what has gone before. What happens is but a consequence of what has already happened.

Such a world could not, to any god contemplating it and capable of understanding it, contain any surprises. Nothing, in short, would ever be created in such a world. There would be novelties of sorts — for example, a snowflake that resembled no other — but these would not be creations in any sense. They would be but novel combinations of what already existed and then pointlessly fell into those combinations. That lifeless world, in short, resembles a clockwork, but one from which the moving hands are missing. What interests us about a clock is that it tells time, but the lifeless world we are now imagining tells us nothing of the sort. On the contrary, the very image of it is enough to exclude considerations of time. A god would discover nothing from the prolonged contemplation of such a world other than what he already knew, and what he could anticipate in it would be nothing not already implicit in his memories of it. Time, to be sure, would exist for such a god — otherwise his contemplation could not be prolonged, nor would it make sense to speak of his memories. But then, by introducing such a being we have, of course, abandoned our premise of a lifeless world.

LIFE AND TIME

Let us next, then, add to this lifeless world, in our imaginations, the whole of living creation, excluding only rational beings, that is to say, beings like ourselves who are in the broadest sense capable not only of understanding but also of creative thought and action. What we have now is still a world without history. Except for the long and gradual changes wrought by biological evolution, nothing new or different occurs in this world. The sun that rises one day illuminates nothing that was not there the day before, or a thousand or million days before. It is simply the same world, age after age. The things in it exactly resemble those that went before. Every sparrow is just like every other, does exactly the same things in the same way without innovation, then to be imitated by every sparrow to follow. The robin or squirrel you see today does nothing different from those you saw as a child, and could be interchanged with them without discernible difference. Each creature arises and lives out its cycle with an invariance that is almost as fixed as the clockwork we imagined a moment ago, and it is, again, a clockwork without hands. That such a creature should live today or a hundred years hence makes no difference. There are days in this world, but no dates. And each such creature then perishes, leaving behind it nothing whatsoever except more of the same kind, which will do the same things again, and beget the same, these unchanging cycles then to be repeated over and over, forever.

THE SENSE OF TIME

The introduction of living things into our imaginary world has, however, resulted in one significant difference, and that is, the rudimentary *sense* of time, at least among some creatures. Irrational beings do not, of course, contemplate in thought their own graves, reflectively make provision for their descendants, mark anniversaries and so on, but they must nevertheless sometimes feel time's passage. A trapped animal feels its life ebbing and senses the approach of death, and perhaps birds, however mechanical or instinctive their behavior may be, have some anticipation of what is going to be done with the nests they build. Our pets anticipate their meals and look forward to them, and possibly the hours drag for them when we leave them alone for the day.

So to that extent time has, in a significant sense, been introduced into our world by the addition to it of living things. But there still remains this huge difference: these creatures have no history. Each does today what was done by those that went before, and will be done by those to come. The world we are imagining thus resembles an endless play in which the acts are all identical. Every stage setting is the same as every other, the lines spoken are the same, the costumes the same, and the things done the same. Only the actors change, but none introduces any innovation. It would make no difference to any audience which act they saw, nor would there be any point in numbering the acts, or noting which followed which.

The world just described is not, of course, an imaginary one. It is the very world we live in, considered independently of ourselves and our place in it. It is a world in which there is a before and after — the sun, for example, must have risen in order to set — and it is one in which the passage of time is felt. Yet it is timeless in another significant sense — it has neither history nor meaning. Its meaninglessness is precisely the meaninglessness of the play we were just imagining. There is never anything new, no purpose, no goal; in a word, nothing is ever created.

AN ANCIENT IMAGE OF MEANINGLESSNESS

This sense of eternal meaninglessness was perfectly captured by the ancients in the myth of Sisyphus. Sisyphus, it will be recalled, was condemned by the gods to roll a stone to the top of a hill, whereupon it would roll back to the bottom, to be moved to the top once more by Sisyphus, then to roll back again, and so on, over and over, throughout eternity. Here, surely, is existence reduced to utter meaninglessness. Nor does that lack of meaning arise from the onerousness of Sisyphus' task. It would not be redeemed if the task were made easier, by representing the stone as a very small one, for example. Nor does that meaninglessness emerge from the sheer boredom of the task. It would still be there even if we imagined Sisyphus to rejoice in it — if we imagined, for example, that he had a compulsive and insatiable desire to roll stones, and considered himself blessed to be able to do this forever.

The meaninglessness exhibited in this myth is precisely the meaninglessness of the world as it has been described up to this point, namely, that of a world without history, a world that is in this significant sense devoid of time. It is, like the cycles of Sisyphus, a world of endless and pointless repetition.

THE EMERGENCE OF MEANING

If we now modify the story of Sisyphus in certain ways we can take the crucial step needed to transform it from an image of meaninglessness to one of meaning. In so doing, we can finally see what is needed to give the world and human existence, or the life of any individual person, meaning.

Let us first suppose, then, that Sisyphus does not roll the same stone over and over again to the top, but moves a different stone each time, each stone then remaining at the top of the hill. Does this make a difference? Hardly. One stone does not differ from another, so what Sisyphus is now doing is essentially what he was doing before, rolling a stone, over and over, to the top of a hill. The stones, for all we know, merely accumulate there as a huge and growing pile of rubble.

So let us next imagine that this is not so, that the stones, having been moved to the top of the hill, are one by one, over a long period of time, assembled, not by Sisyphus but by others, into something beautiful and lasting — a great temple, we might suppose. Has Sisyphus' existence now gained meaning? In a sense it has, for his labor is no longer wasted and pointless. Something important does come of it all. But that existence might still be totally meaningless to

Sisyphus, for what we have imagined is consistent with supposing that he is totally ignorant of what is happening, that he is aware only of rolling stones, one after the other endlessly, with no notion at all of what becomes of them, the temple being entirely the work of others and out of his sight and ken. From his point of view, then, nothing has changed at all.

We next imagine, then, that this latter is not so, that Sisyphus sees the fruit of his toil gradually take shape, is aware of its importance and beauty, and thus has at least the satisfaction of understanding what is happening and realizing that what he does is not totally in vain. Something important does come of it all, something that is great and beautiful, and it is something that is understood.

Now have we invested his existence with meaning? In a sense we have, for Sisyphus has been converted from a mere beast of burden to a being who understands. But there is still a lot missing. For what we now have before us is consistent with the idea that Sisyphus is a mere slave, a rational slave up to a point, to be sure, but still one who goes through endless and repetitive motions over which he has no choice, these being entirely dictated by others, and for a result in which he has no choice, but can only passively observe. To revert to our image of the endlessly repetitive stage play, Sisyphus is here like an actor whose luck is to be cast in the leading role, but with this difference: an actor can at least reject the role. Such an existence is not without fulfillment of a sort, but we must remember that it still corresponds to the meaningless and, in a significant sense, timeless existence into which the whole of animal creation is cast. The vast array of living cycles today resemble those of a thousand years ago, and will resemble those of a thousand years hence. Nature, so conceived, is not without grandeur and beauty, just as we can imagine the temple that rises from Sisyphus' labors to have the same qualities. But that image still lacks an essential ingredient of meaningfulness, unless, of course, we are willing to ascribe a fully meaningful existence to a merely productive machine, or to a slave who has no voice whatsoever in his own fate or even his own actions from one moment to the next.

One final modification is needed, then, and that is to imagine that Sisyphus not only moves this prodigious quantity of stones to the top of the hill, but that he does so for the very purpose of seeing them converted to a beautiful and lasting temple. Most important of all, this temple must be something of his own, the product of his own creative mind, of his own conception, something which, but for his own creative thought and imagination, would never have existed at all.

CREATION, MEANING, AND TIME

It is at this point, then, that the idea of a fully meaningful existence emerges, for the first time. It is inseparable from the concept of creativity. And it is exactly this that was missing from everything we have imagined up until now. Nature, however beautiful and awesome, exhibits nothing of creative activity until we include in it rational beings, that is, beings who can think, imagine, plan, and execute things of worth, beings who are, in the true sense, originators or creators. Rational beings do not merely foresee what will be; they sometimes determine what will be. They do not, like the rest of creation, merely wait to see what nature will thrust upon them. They sometimes impose upon nature herself their own creations, sometimes creations of great and lasting significance. Rational beings are the very creators of time itself, in the historical sense, for without them there would be only a meaningless succession of things and no history at all. An animal can, perhaps, anticipate its own death, as can a person, and an animal can bring about works, sometimes of considerable beauty and complexity, as can a person. But what the animal thus does has been done in exactly that way millions of times before. One thinks of the complex beauty of the spider's web, the intricate basketry of the oriole's nest, the ingenious construction of the honeycomb — all things of impressive intricacy, sometimes arresting and marvelous, but also things that disclose not the least hint of creative power. They are, like Sisyphus' labors, only endless repetitions. Human beings, or at least some of them, are capable of going a crucial step further. What a creative mind brings forth is never something merely learned or inherited, nor is it merely something novel, like the snowflake that resembles no other. It is what a creative mind intends it to be, something to which the notions of success or failure can apply, and sometimes something of such extraordinary originality that no other man or god, no one but its creator himself, could ever have foreseen. And if that creative mind possesses, in addition to this, the rare quality of creative genius, then what is wrought is not merely something that others could neither do nor foresee, it is something they could not even imagine. Thus we see the aptness of Schopenhauer's dictum, that while talent is the ability to hit a target that others miss, genius is the ability to hit a target that others do not even see.

The ancients, in their philosophies, were fond of describing their gods as rational. This idea of divine rationality has persisted among metaphysicians, but the concept of rationality has become narrowed. We think of rationality as care and precision in thought, a due regard for evidence and consistency, and sometimes as mere restraint in conduct. But the ancients quite properly associated it with the contemplative life in the broadest sense. The creation of things beautiful, profound, and unprecedented expressed for them the essence of human rationality. Sisyphus displayed his ultimate rationality, not merely in understanding what he was doing — something that would be within the power of a mere slave — but, as we have modified the myth, in the display of strength and genius that took the form of a beautiful and lasting temple, born first in his own imagination. That was something that no mere slave, and indeed no mere human being, and in fact no other being under the sun except this one could ever have done. The creative genius of a particular person is something that by its very nature cannot be shared. To the extent that it is shared, such that what it brings forth is also brought forth by others, then it is not only not genius, it is not even a creative power. It is but the capacity for fabrication which, however striking it may be, is quite common throughout nature.

THE CREATION OF THINGS GREAT AND SMALL

Lest the impression be given that the creative thought and work that I am here praising is something rare, the possession of only a few, let it be noted that it exists in degrees and is, in one form or another, far from rare. What is rare is, I think, the proper appreciation of it. We tend to think of creative works as spectacular achievements, particularly in the arts, but in fact the human capacity to create something new is sometimes found in quite mundane things. Thus, for example, the establishment of a brilliant position in a game of chess is a perfect example of creativity, even though the result is of little value. Things as common as gardening, woodworking, and the like give scope to the originality of those who have the knack for them, and are probably the most constant source of life's joys. Intelligent, perhaps witty conversation, and the composition of clear and forceful prose are just as good examples of creativity as the making of a poem of great beauty or depth of meaning, however much they may differ in worth. Another example of a creative work, and one whose value as a creation is rarely appreciated, is the raising of a beautiful family, something that is reserved for the relatively few who can, as a natural gift, do it well. Of course the mere begetting of children is no act of creation at all. It is something that can be done by anyone. And other creatures sometimes with great skill convert their young to self-sufficient adults. They succeed, however, only to the extent that these young exactly resemble themselves, whereas rational human parents should measure their success by the degree to which their children become self-sufficient and capable adults who do *not* resemble their parents, but express instead their own individualities. This is an art that is neither common nor easily learned.

OPPOSING CONCEPTIONS
OF MEANINGFUL EXISTENCE

It would be gratifying if, in the light of what I have been saying, we could now rest upon the comfortable conclusion that our lives derive their meaning from the fact that human beings, and they alone, impose a history upon nature, that the world does not merely persist from age to age, nor does it merely change in the manner of the endless recurrences we see throughout the rest of creation, but that changes are imposed upon it by the creative power of humankind.

That would be true, but too general, for, in truth, creative power is not something particularly sought and prized by most people. Our culture has taught us to regard all persons as of equal worth, and our religion tells us that this is even God's estimate. Indeed, we are taught that we are, each and every one, created in the very image of that God, so that no one can claim for himself more importance than anyone else. Our lives, it is implied, are invested with great meaning just by virtue of our common humanity. We need only to be born, and our worth is once and for all assured. We are, to be sure, set apart from the remainder of creation, according to this tradition, but what sets us apart is not necessarily anything we do. We are set apart by what is merely given to us, so that a human life, and a valuable and meaningful life, are presumed to be one and the same.

That conception of meaningful existence, which is so familiar, omits the essential ingredient of meaningfulness. For, in truth, creative power is no common possession. Creative genius is in fact rare. The work of the vast majority of persons does not deviate much from what others have already done and from what can be found everywhere. There seems even to be a determination in most people that this should be so, a determination to pattern their lives after others, to seek as little originality and individual self-worth as possible. People tend, like apes, to mimic and imitate what they already find, absorbing the ideas, manners, values, even, indeed, their religions, from those around them, as if by osmosis. They appropriate virtually everything, returning virtually nothing of their own creative power. The lives of most persons are like the clockwork alluded to previously. They are born, pass through the several stages of life, indulging, for the most part, in only trivial thoughts and feelings, absorbing pleasures and distractions, fleeing boredom, conceiving no significant works, and leaving almost nothing behind them. It would be sad enough if this were merely so. What is far sadder is that it is thought not really to matter. Religion then reinforces this by proclaiming that no one can, in God's sight, rise above others anyway, that the fool is already as blessed as the wise, and that the greatest possible human worth has already been bestowed upon us all by our merely being born. It is a hard notion to overcome, and weighs upon us like lead. It tends to render even the exemplary among us weak and hesitant.

We take much comfort in that part of the Bible, the very first book, which assures us that we are all the veritable images of God. We tend to overlook the first five words with which the Bible begins: "In the beginning, God created . . ." That the result of that act is heaven and earth may be overwhelming, but the emphasis is wrong if we dwell on that. What is significant is that the original description of God is as a *creator*. And it is this, surely, that endows one with the divine quality. That human beings exist is not, in itself, a significant fact. That this or that being is possessed of human form, or is of that biological species, is likewise of no significance, whatever may be the teaching of religion and custom to the contrary. What *is* significant, what gives any human existence its meaning, is the possibility that out of this existence arises creative power. But it is no more than a possibility, realized here and there, more or less, and fully realized only in exceptional persons.

IN PRAISE OF GREATNESS

One brings to consciousness the indescribable worth of creative power by imagining specific instances. Consider, for example, that on a given day the sun rose, as usual, and that throughout that day most of the world was much as it had been the day before, virtually all of its inhabitants doing more or less what they were accustomed to doing; but, in a minute part of that world, a nocturne of Chopin's came into being, or a sonata of Mozart's. On another day, otherwise much like any other, Lincoln composed his address for the visit to Gettysburg, or, Mathew Arnold wrote the concluding lines of his *Dover Beach*, or Grey his *Elegy*, or Plato his *Symposium*. That a little-known woman gave birth to an infant in Malaga, Spain, one October day in 1881 means very little, but that the child was to become Picasso means much. And to complete this kind of imaginative exercise, one needs to fix in his thought some significant creation — something, perhaps, as small but priceless as a prelude of Chopin or a poem of Keats — and then realize that, if a particular person had not at just that moment brought forth that utterly unprecedented thing, then it would never have existed at all. The thought of a world altogether devoid of music or literature or art is the thought of a world that is dark indeed, but if one dwells on it, the thought of a world lacking a single one of the fruits of creative genius that our world actually possesses is a depressing one. That such a world would have been so easy, so inevitable, but for a solitary person, at a single moment, is a shattering reflection.

This vision of greatness is as old as philosophy. One wishes it were the theme of religion as well, for the voice of religion is always louder than that of philosophy. That a world should exist is not finally important, nor does it mean much, by itself, that people should inhabit it. But that some of these should, in varying degrees, be capable of creating worlds of their own and history — thereby creating time in its historical sense — is what gives our lives whatever meaning they have.

For Further Reading

CHAPTER 1: THE NEED FOR METAPHYSICS

SCHOPENHAUER, A., "On Man's Need of Metaphysics," *The Will to Live*, ed. Richard Taylor. New York: Frederick Ungar Publishing Co., 1967.

CHAPTER 2: PERSONS AND BODIES

AQUINAS, ST. THOMAS, "Man: His Powers; His Knowledge," *Introduction to St. Thomas Aquinas*, ed. Anton C. Pegis. New York: Modern Library, Inc., 1948.

PLATO, *Phaedo, The Dialogues of Plato*, tr. B. Jowett. New York: Random House, 1937.

RYLE, GILBERT, *The Concept of Mind*. London: Hutchinson's University Library, 1949.

WISDOM, JOHN, *Problems of Mind and Matter*, Chapters 1–3. New York: Cambridge University Press, 1970.

CHAPTER 3: INTERACTIONISM

DESCARTES, R., *Passions of the Soul*, Part I, *Meditations*, particularly 1, 2, and 6, in *Descartes: Selections*, ed. R.M. Eaton. New York: Charles Scribner's Sons, 1927.

DUCASSE, C.J., *Nature, Mind and Death*, particularly Chapters 12, 14, 17, and 18. La Salle, Ill.: The Open Court Publishing Company, 1951.

VESEY, G.N.A., *The Embodied Mind*. London: George Allen & Unwin Ltd., 1965.

WISDOM, JOHN, *Problems of Mind and Matter,* Chapters 4–7. New York: Cambridge University Press, 1970.

CHAPTER 4: THE MIND AS A FUNCTION OF THE BODY

ARMSTRONG, D.M., *A Materialist Theory of the Mind.* New York: Humanities Press, 1968.

HOBBES, THOMAS, *The Metaphysical System of Hobbes,* selected by Mary Whiton Calkins. La Salle, Ill.: The Open Court Publishing Company, 1948.

JAMES, WILLIAM, "The Automaton Theory," *The Principles of Psychology.* New York: Holt, Rinehart & Winston, Inc., 1890.

O'CONNOR, JOHN, *Modern Materialism.* New York: Harcourt Brace Jovanovich, 1969.

CHAPTER 5: FREEDOM AND DETERMINISM

AYER, A.J., "Freedom and Necessity," *Philosophical Essays.* London: Macmillan & Company, Ltd., 1954.

BEROFSKY, BERNARD, *Free Will and Determinism.* New York: Harper & Row, 1966.

CAMPBELL, C.A., "Has the Self 'Free Will'?" *Selfhood and Godhood.* London: George Allen & Unwin Ltd., 1957.

FICHTE, J.G., "Doubt," *The Vocation of Man.* New York: Liberal Arts Press, Inc., 1956.

HOOK, SIDNEY, ed. *Determinism and Freedom in the Age of Modern Science.* New York: New York University Press, 1958.

HUME, DAVID, "Of Liberty and Necessity," *An Enquiry Concerning Human Understanding.* New York: Liberal Arts Press, Inc., 1955.

JAMES, WILLIAM, "The Dilemma of Determinism," *The Will to Believe and Other Essays.* New York: Longmans, Green & Co., Inc., 1927.

RYLE, GILBERT, "The Will," *The Concept of Mind.* London: Hutchinson's University Library, 1949.

TAYLOR, RICHARD, *Action and Purpose.* Englewood Cliffs, N.J.: Prentice-Hall, Inc., 1965.

CHAPTER 6: FATE

ARISTOTLE, "De Interpretatione," *The Basic Works of Aristotle,* ed. Richard McKeon. New York: Random House, 1941.

BOETHIUS, *The Consolation of Philosophy,* Book V, tr. W.V. Cooper. New York: Modern Library, Inc., 1943.

CAHN, STEVEN M., *Fate, Logic and Time*. New Haven: Yale University Press, 1967.

CICERO, *De Fato*, tr. H. Rackham. Cambridge: Loeb Classical Library, Harvard University Press, 1960.

RYLE, GILBERT, "It Was to Be," *Dilemmas*. New York: Cambridge University Press, 1954.

CHAPTER 7: SPACE AND TIME

McTAGGART, J.M.E., "The Unreality of Time," *Philosophical Studies*. London: Edward Arnold & Co., 1934.

MOORE, G.E., "Is Time Unreal?" *Some Main Problems of Philosophy*. London: George Allen & Unwin Ltd., 1953.

SMART, J.J.C., ed., *Problems of Space and Time*. New York, Macmillan & Company, Inc., 1964.

CHAPTER 8: THE RELATIVITY OF SPACE AND TIME

BLACK, MAX, "The Direction of Time," *Models and Metaphors*. Ithaca, New York: Cornell University Press, 1962.

EDDINGTON, A.S., *Space, Time and Gravitation*. Cambridge: Cambridge University Press, 1920.

LEIBNIZ, GOTTRRIED, "The Relational Theory of Space and Time," *Problems of Space and Time*, ed. J.J.C. Smart. New York: Macmillan & Company, Inc., 1964.

SCHLICK, MORITZ, *Philosophy of Nature*, Chapter 7. New York: Philosophical Library, 1949.

CHAPTER 9: TEMPORAL PASSAGE

AUGUSTINE, ST., *Confessions*, Book XI. London: Everyman's Library, J.M. Dent & Sons, Ltd., 1949.

GOODMAN, NELSON, *The Structure of Appearance*, Chapter XI. Cambridge, Mass.: Harvard University Press, 1951.

QUINE, W.V., *Word and Object*, Section 36. Cambridge, Mass.: John Wiley & Sons, Inc., 1960.

SMART, J.J.C., "The River of Time, *Essays in Conceptual Analysis*, ed. A.G.N. Flew. London: Macmillan & Company, Ltd., 1956.

CHAPTER 10: CAUSATION

BLANSHARD, BRAND, *Reason and Analysis*. La Salle, Ill.: The Open Court Publishing Co., 1962.

HUME, DAVID, "Of the Idea of Necessary Connection," *An Enquiry Concerning Human Understanding*. New York: The Liberal Arts Press, 1955.

TAYLOR, RICHARD, *Action and Purpose*. Englewood Cliffs, N.J.: Prentice-Hall, Inc., 1965.

CHAPTER 11: GOD

AQUINAS, ST. THOMAS, "God," *Introduction to St. Thomas Aquinas*, ed. Anton C. Pegis. New York: Modern Library, Inc., 1948.

GILSON, E., *The Christian Philosophy of St. Thomas Aquinas*, Part I. London: Victor Gollancz, Ltd., 1957.

HICK, JOHN, ed. *The Existence of God*. Ithaca, N.Y.: Cornell University Press, 1965.

HUME, DAVID, *Dialogues Concerning Natural Religion*, ed. Norman Kemp Smith. Oxford: The Clarendon Press, 1935.

LEIBNIZ, G.W., "On the Ultimate Origination of Things," *The Monadology and Other Philosophical Writings*, ed. Robert Latta. London: Oxford University Press, 1948.

CHAPTER 12: POLARITY

BERGSON, HENRI, *An Introduction to Metaphysics*, tr. T.E. Hulme. Indianapolis: Bobbs-Merrill Co., 1949.

JAMES, WILLIAM, "Bergson and his Critique of Intellectualism," *A Pluralistic Universe*. New York: Longmans, Green & Co., 1920.

JAMES, WILLIAM, *Some Problems of Philosophy*. New York: Longmans, Green & Co., 1911.

PUCCETTI, ROLAND, "Brain Transplantation and Personal Identity," *Analysis*, 1969.

CHAPTER 13: METAPHYSICS AND MEANING

HANFLING, OSWALD, *The Quest for Meaning*. Oxford: Basil Blackwell, Ltd., 1987.

SCHOPENHAUER, ARTHUR, "On the Vanity and Suffering of Existence," *Essays and Aphorisms*, tr. R.J. Hollingdale. New York: Penguin Classics, 1970.

TAYLOR, RICHARD, "Happiness," *Ethics, Faith and Reason*. Englewood Cliffs, N.J.: Prentice-Hall, Inc., 1985.

Index